BLACKSTONE OUTDOOR

GAS GRIDDLE BIBLE

IMPRESS EVERYONE WITH YOUR GRIDDLE SKILLS – OVER 2000
DAYS OF SIMPLE, SWIFT, AND SAVORY RECIPES PLUS SECRET TIPS
FOR SIZZLING SUCCESS ALL YEAR!

Paul J. Baker

_____

THANK YOU FOR PURCHASING MY BOOK!
IF YOU ENJOYED IT, I WOULD APPRECIATE YOUR HONEST
FEEDBACK ON AMAZON

_____

If you have any concerns, please email me at:
info@topqualitybooks.com
I want to create high-quality products that give everyone satisfaction

TABLE OF CONTENTS

WELCOME TO THE BLACKSTONE FAMILY

Welcome to the exciting world of outdoor cooking, where the aroma of grilled food blends seamlessly with the fresh air of the outdoors, creating an inviting atmosphere for family and friends. If you're new to this scene, you're in for a treat, especially with a Blackstone griddle as your culinary companion. In this chapter, we'll dive into the history of outdoor griddles and explore how they have evolved into the modern-day marvels we know today, focusing on the exceptional features of the Blackstone griddle.

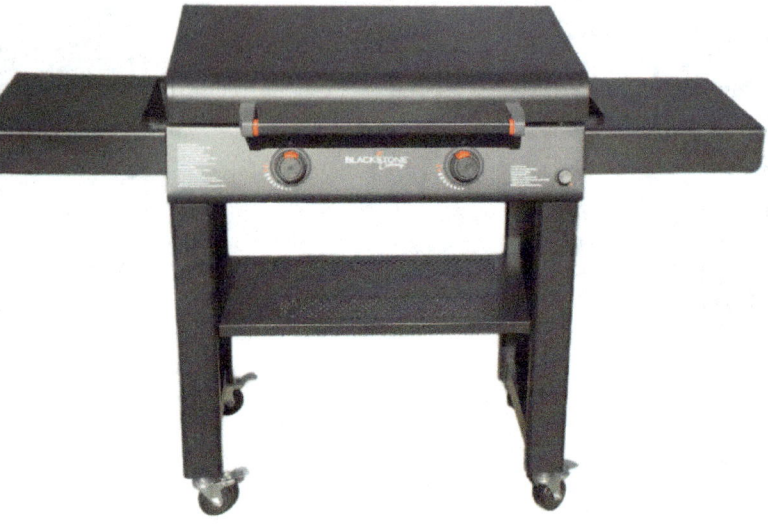

A Brief History of Outdoor Cooking

The concept of cooking over an open flame is as old as civilization, beginning with the discovery of fire. Early humans quickly realized that food tasted better and was easier to digest when cooked. As centuries passed, the methods and tools for outdoor cooking evolved from simple campfires to sophisticated cooking apparatuses designed to enhance flavor and convenience.

In the past, outdoor cooking was often reserved for campsites and picnics, utilizing portable grills and makeshift setups. However, as people began to appreciate the joy and communal spirit of cooking and eating outdoors, the demand for more permanent and practical solutions grew. This led to the development of various outdoor cooking technologies, including the outdoor griddle.

The Rise of Outdoor Griddles

Outdoor griddles have transformed outdoor cooking by providing a versatile and efficient platform beyond traditional grilling. Unlike standard grills that often feature open grates, griddles provide a flat cooking surface, which expands the variety of foods you can prepare outdoors. The griddle accommodates everything from pancakes and eggs to stir-fries and smash burgers.

Introducing the Blackstone Griddle

The Blackstone griddle represents the pinnacle of outdoor griddle design, offering robust construction and innovative features that cater to both novice and seasoned chefs.

With its solid steel cooking surface, the Blackstone griddle distributes heat evenly, ensuring perfectly cooked meals every time. Its simplicity of use and excellence of performance have made it a favorite among outdoor cooking enthusiasts.

Why Choose Blackstone?

Choosing a Blackstone griddle means opting for versatility and quality. Whether you're hosting a backyard barbecue, cooking a family breakfast on the patio, or tailgating at a sports event, the Blackstone turns any gathering into a culinary event. Its ease of use and ability to cook almost anything makes it an indispensable tool for anyone who loves to cook outdoors.

Additionally, Blackstone griddles are designed with the user in mind, featuring easy ignition systems, adjustable heat controls, and a grease management system that makes cleanup a breeze. These user-friendly features ensure that your focus remains on the cooking and the company, not the cleanup.

Evolving with the Times

As outdoor lifestyles continue to gain popularity, the Blackstone griddle has kept pace with the times, incorporating features that today's outdoor cooks need. From portable models that fit in the trunk of a car to larger, more elaborate setups that are the centerpiece of an outdoor kitchen, Blackstone offers a range of products to suit any outdoor cooking requirement.

In conclusion, the evolution of outdoor griddles has mirrored the changes in our social and culinary landscapes. With its blend of traditional cooking methods and modern technology, the Blackstone griddle stands as a testament to this evolution, offering a versatile and enjoyable way to reconnect with the joy of outdoor cooking. Whether you are a novice looking to explore the world of outdoor griddles or a seasoned chef aiming to refine your outdoor culinary skills, the Blackstone griddle is your gateway to a new world of flavors and experiences.

In the next section, we'll discuss selecting the perfect Blackstone model to suit your outdoor cooking needs, ensuring you make the most of your griddle from the first use.

Choosing the Right Model: A Buyer's Guide

Given the variety of options available, selecting the right Blackstone griddle model can be as exciting as daunting. Each model has specific features to cater to different cooking needs and preferences. Whether you're a seasoned grill master or a casual weekend chef, understanding each model's key features and differences will help you make an informed decision. Here's a comprehensive guide to help you navigate your choices and find the perfect Blackstone griddle for outdoor cooking adventures.

Assessing Your Needs

Before diving into the specifics of each model, consider how you plan to use your griddle:

- **Frequency of use**: Will you use it occasionally or daily?
- **Types of meals**: Are you looking to cook breakfasts, complete dinners, or both?
- **Number of people**: Are you cooking for your family or large gatherings?
- **Portability**: Do you need something to bring on camping trips or tailgates?
- **Space**: How much outdoor space is available for cooking and storage?

Model Variations and Features

1. The Classic Range

- <u>Blackstone 28" Griddle</u>: Ideal for small to medium-sized families, the 28" model offers two independently controlled burners and a substantial 470 square inches of cooktop. It's compact enough for smaller patios but capable of cooking a full meal.
- <u>Blackstone 36" Griddle</u>: The 36" model is perfect for those who frequently host large gatherings. With four adjustable heat zones, you get an expansive 720 square inches of cooking surface, allowing for versatile cooking options and the ability to simultaneously cook several types of food.

2. The Adventure-Ready Range

- <u>Blackstone Adventure Ready 17" Tabletop Griddle</u>: This model is designed for the great outdoors. It is compact and easily portable, offering 267 square inches of cooking space and a single H-style burner. It's perfect for camping, tailgating, or anywhere your adventures might take you.
- <u>Blackstone Adventure Ready 22" Griddle with Stand</u>: Slightly more significant than the 17" model, this griddle provides two H-style burners and 339 square inches of cooking area. It has a stand and is still portable enough to move around quickly.

3. The Culinary Collection

- <u>Blackstone 36" Air Fryer Griddle Combo</u>: This model features a spacious griddle and includes air frying and warming drawers, making it the ultimate cooking station.

Must-Have Accessories for Every Blackstone Owner

Owning a Blackstone griddle opens up a world of culinary possibilities, but having the right accessories can further enhance your cooking experience. Whether grilling steaks, flipping pancakes, or preparing a vegetable stir-fry, these must-have accessories will make your griddle cooking more efficient, enjoyable, and versatile.

1. Griddle Tool Kit

A basic griddle tool kit is indispensable. It typically includes long spatulas perfect for flipping burgers or moving large amounts of food across the griddle surface, tongs for gripping and turning more delicate items, and a chopper/scraper for dicing foods or cleaning the griddle after use. Look for kits that offer high-quality stainless steel tools with heat-resistant handles to ensure durability and comfort.

2. Basting Cover

A basting cover is crucial for melting cheese on burgers, steaming vegetables, or even cooking eggs perfectly on the griddle. It helps trap heat and steam to speed up cooking and infuse flavors, making it easier to manage your cooking temperature and moisture levels. Choose a cover that's large enough to cover multiple items but light enough to handle easily.

3. Grease Cup Liners

To simplify cleanup, invest in disposable grease cup liners. These liners fit into your Blackstone's grease tray, making grease disposal quick and clean. They are instrumental during long cooking sessions or when preparing greasy foods like bacon or sausages.

4. Griddle Cleaning Kit

Proper maintenance of your Blackstone griddle ensures its longevity and performance. A griddle cleaning kit typically includes the following:

- A scraper for removing cooked-on residue.
- Cleaning pads for scrubbing the griddle surface.
- A cleaning solution formulated explicitly for griddle care.

Regularly using these tools will keep your griddle surface in prime condition and ready for your next barbecue.

5. Hard Cover or Soft Cover

Protecting your Blackstone griddle from the elements is vital, especially if you store it outdoors. A hard cover provides sturdy protection against rain, snow, and dirt, while a soft cover is usually lighter, easier to handle, and great for shielding the griddle from dust and light moisture. Depending on your storage conditions, choose a cover that offers adequate protection and fits your griddle model snugly.

6. Cutting Board

A high-quality cutting board designed to fit securely on your griddle station can streamline your cooking process by allowing you to chop and slice ingredients right where you cook them. Look for a cutting board that can withstand heat and is durable enough to handle heavy use.

7. Thermometer

A good thermometer is essential for precision cooking, especially for meats. Instant-read digital thermometers or infrared thermometers designed for surface readings can help you cook your food at the perfect temperature, ensuring delicious and safe meals every time.

8. Griddle Warming Rack

A warming rack is invaluable for large cooking sessions. It keeps freshly cooked items warm while you finish cooking other dishes. It's perfect for managing meal components and ensures that everything comes to the table hot and ready to enjoy.

9. Breakfast Kit

For those who love starting their day with a hearty breakfast cooked outdoors, a breakfast kit with specialized accessories like pancake dispensers, egg rings, and a bacon press will enhance your morning meal routine.

By equipping yourself with these essential accessories, your Blackstone griddle will become more than just a cooking appliance; it will be a complete outdoor kitchen that allows you to unleash your culinary creativity. Each accessory adds convenience and expands the kinds of dishes you can prepare, making every griddle session a new adventure.

Setup and Safety Essentials

Proper setup is crucial for safe operation and optimal performance. This step-by-step guide will walk you through assembling and preparing your Blackstone griddle for its first use, ensuring you start on the right foot.

Step-by-Step Setup Guide

1. Unboxing and Assembly

- **Check All Parts**: Before assembling your griddle, ensure all parts are present. Check against the included parts list to ensure everything is present and intact.
- **Assemble According to Instructions**: Follow the assembly instructions carefully. Most Blackstone griddles require attaching the legs, setting up the cooking surface, and connecting the burners. Use the correct tools as specified in the manual, and make sure all screws and bolts are tight for stability.
- **Positioning**: Place your griddle in a well-ventilated, stable area away from combustible materials. Ensure the surface is level to avoid uneven cooking and oil pooling.

2. Connecting the Propane Tank

- **Safety First**: Before attaching the propane tank, please ensure all griddle controls are in the 'OFF' position.
- **Check for Leaks**: After connecting the propane tank, apply a soapy water solution to the connection points. Turn on the gas slightly. If you see bubbles forming, there is a gas leak. Could you tighten the connections and test again? If leaks continue, do not use the griddle and contact customer service.
- **Secure the Tank**: Once securely connected and checked for leaks, place the propane tank where it won't be tipped over or subjected to heat.

3. Seasoning the Griddle

- **Clean the Surface**: Before you use your griddle for the first time, wash the cooking surface with warm, soapy water to remove any residues from the manufacturing process. Rinse thoroughly and dry.
- **Heat It**: Turn the burners to medium-high and heat the griddle until it darkens 10 to 15 minutes.
- **Apply Oil**: Use a high smoke point oil (like flaxseed, canola, or vegetable oil). Using a paper towel held with tongs, apply a thin, even layer across the entire surface. Be careful, as the griddle will be hot.
- **Smoke and Cure**: The oil will begin to smoke. Allow it to smoke off; this process polymerizes the oil, creating a non-stick coating. Repeat this oiling and heating process 3-4 times to build an excellent initial seasoning layer.
- **Cool Down**: Turn off the griddle and let it cool completely.

4. Safety Guidelines

- **Regular Checks**: Before each use, check for gas leaks and inspect the hose for abrasions or leaks.
- **Supervision**: Never leave the griddle unattended while in use. Keep children and pets away from the cooking area.
- **Proper Utensils**: Use long-handled, heat-resistant griddle tools to avoid burns.
- **Fire Safety**: Keep a fire extinguisher rated for grease fires nearby in case of emergencies.
- **Ventilation**: Always use your griddle outdoors in a well-ventilated area to prevent carbon monoxide buildup.

Setting up your Blackstone griddle correctly ensures safety and enhances your cooking experience. I'd like you to please take the time to familiarize yourself with the process and your equipment. Following these guidelines ensures that every meal cooked on your new griddle is delicious and prepared safely. Enjoy the endless possibilities that your Blackstone griddle offers.

Connecting Your Blackstone Griddle to an RV Propane Line

A Blackstone griddle can significantly enhance your cooking experience whenenjoying the great outdoors with your RV. Many RVs come with an outdoor kitchen that includes a built-in propane line, which can be a convenient power source for your griddle. This chapter will guide you through connecting your Blackstone griddle to your RV's propane system, making outdoor cooking more accessible and more enjoyable.

Understanding the Setup

When you purchase a Blackstone griddle, it typically comes with a pressure regulator designed for use with portable propane tanks. These tiny tanks are great for occasional use but can run out quickly, which is frustrating during longer cooking sessions. An RV's built-in propane system offers a more stable and enduring supply thanks to larger tank capacities and the convenience of a fixed system.

Necessary Equipment

To connect your Blackstone griddle to your RV's propane line, you will need a couple of specific items:

1. **Propane Hose**: This is the conduit that will connect your griddle to the RV's propane outlet. An adequate hose is essential to reach your RV, where you'll cook safely.
2. **Propane Adapter**: This fitting is crucial because it lets you connect the hose to your griddle without using its standard pressure regulator.

Step-by-Step Connection Guide

1. **Remove the Pressure Regulator**: The regulator that comes with your Blackstone griddle is designed for small, portable propane tanks and unsuitable for an RV's built-in system, which has its regulator. Using both regulators together can impede gas flow and reduce heat output.
2. **Attach the Adapter**: Screw the adapter into the input where the regulator was initially connected on your griddle. Ensure it is tightened securely but not overtightened, which could damage the threads.
3. **Connect the Hose**: Attach one end of your propane hose to the adapter you've just installed on the griddle. Make sure the connection is secure.
4. **Hook Up to the RV**: Connect the other end of the hose to the RV's propane line output. Again, ensure this connection is tight and secure to prevent any leaks.
5. **Check for Leaks**: Before using the griddle, it's essential to check for any gas leaks. You can do this by applying a soapy water solution to the connections. There is a leak if bubbles form when the propane is turned on. Tighten the connections and check again.
6. **Test the Setup**: Turn on the propane from the RV and ignite the griddle according to the manufacturer's instructions. You should notice that the griddle heats up quickly to the desired cooking temperature.

Tips for Optimal Use

- **Cover Your Griddle**: Invest in a Blackstone cover to protect your griddle from outdoor elements. This will help maintain its condition and functionality.
- **Always Monitor**: When your griddle is connected to the RV's propane line, keep an eye on it while cooking. This will ensure safety and help you manage the cooking temperatures effectively.
- **Regular Maintenance**: Regularly inspect both your griddle and propane connections for wear and potential issues. Proper maintenance will extend the life of both your griddle and the propane setup.

Connecting your Blackstone griddle to your RV's propane line can greatly simplify your cooking process while camping or tailgating. With the right equipment and a bit of setup, you can enjoy endless grilling without worrying about running out of fuel. Happy grilling, and enjoy the convenience of your RV's outdoor kitchen setup!

Seasoning and Reseasoning Your Blackstone Gas Griddle

Seasoning your Blackstone Gas Griddle before its first use is crucial to ensure optimal performance and longevity. This process creates a natural, non-stick coating, prevents rust, promotes even cooking, and facilitates easier food release. Here's a detailed guide to help you properly season your griddle and set a strong foundation for your outdoor cooking adventures.

1. Initial Cleaning
Proper preparation of your griddle's surface is essential for effective seasoning:
- **Wash the Surface**: Thoroughly clean the griddle using warm, soapy water to remove any residues from the manufacturing process, including oils that were applied at the factory to prevent rust during shipping and storage.
- **Rinse and Dry**: Carefully rinse the griddle with clean water to eliminate any soap traces. Dry the surface completely with a clean cloth or paper towel.

2. Heating the Griddle
Prepare the griddle for seasoning by heating it to open the pores of the metal, which helps the oil bond more effectively:
- **Ignite the Burners**: Turn all burners to their highest setting and heat the griddle until it starts changing to dark brown or bronze. This usually takes about 10-15 minutes and indicates the griddle is ready for oiling.

3. Applying the Oil
Choosing the right oil is crucial because high-smoke point oils polymerize best, forming a durable non-stick layer:
- **Oil Selection**: Use oils like flaxseed, canola, vegetable, or shortening for best results.
- **Apply the Oil**: Pour a small amount of oil onto the griddle. Using a paper towel held with tongs, spread it evenly across the entire surface, including the sides and backstop. Ensure the layer is thin to avoid stickiness.
- **Smoke Off the Oil**: As the oil heats, it will begin to smoke, signaling the start of the polymerization process. Allow the griddle to smoke until it ceases, indicating the oil has fully bonded to the surface. This step typically lasts about 10-15 minutes.

4. Repeating the Process
For a robust, non-stick coating, the oiling and heating process should be repeated several times:
- **Cool and Re-oil**: After the initial smoking stops, let the griddle cool slightly, then apply another thin layer of oil. Heat until smoking stops again. Repeat this process 3-4 times to build up a solid layer. The surface should darken and become more polished with each application.

Final Steps and Maintenance
- **Cool Down**: Once the final layer is complete, turn off the griddle and allow it to cool completely. Your Blackstone griddle is now seasoned and ready for use.

- **Maintenance Tips**: After cooking, clean the surface while it is still warm by removing food residues. Apply a light coat of oil to protect the surface before storing. Regular upkeep, such as re-seasoning after deep cleanings or if rust appears, is crucial to maintain the non-stick quality.

Following these detailed steps ensures that your Blackstone griddle is well-seasoned and prepared for many successful cookouts.

When to Reseason Your Griddle
Reseasoning your griddle is necessary to maintain its performance and longevity. Here are situations that call for reasoning:
- **After Cooking Acidic or Sugary Foods**: Foods like tomatoes or teriyaki sauce can break down the seasoning due to their acidity or sugar content, necessitating a fresh layer of oil.
- **When Non-Stick Performance Declines**: If foods start sticking more than usual, it's a sign that the seasoning layer needs replenishment.
- **Visual Changes**: If you notice uneven coloring or bronze patches developing, it's time to add more oil and reheat the griddle to restore the seasoning.

Daily Cleaning and Maintenance Guide

Cleaning your Blackstone Griddle is crucial for maintaining the longevity of your cooking surface and ensuring each meal is as delicious as the last. This chapter will guide you through a straightforward and effective cleaning routine to keep your griddle in top condition.

Importance of Immediate Cleaning

- **Cleaning As You Go**: The key to an easy clean-up is addressing spills and splatters as they occur. This prevents substances from burning onto the surface and becoming difficult to remove later.
- **Managing Heat**: Reduce your griddle's temperature a few minutes before you finish cooking. This decreases the intensity of residual heat, preventing food from burning onto the surface once removed.

Step-by-Step Cleaning Process

- **Let It Cool Slightly**: Let the griddle cool down just enough so it's safe to touch but still warm. This will make it easier to clean food particles and grease.
- **Scrape the Surface**: Using a metal spatula or scraper, gently scrape off any food bits and debris from the surface. Push the residue into the grease trap or wipe it off with a paper towel.
- **Wipe Down**: Wipe the surface with a cloth or paper towel after scraping. For a more thorough clean, use a cloth dipped in warm water.
- **Dry the Surface**: Use a clean cloth or paper towel to dry the griddle completely. This prevents rust and prepares it for subsequent use or storage.

Regular Cleaning Routine

- **Apply Oil**: Once the griddle is clean and dry, apply a light coat of cooking oil to the surface. Use a high smoke point oil like canola or vegetable oil. Spread it evenly with a paper towel or a cloth. This helps maintain the seasoning and protects the griddle from moisture and rust.
- **Check for Rust**: Regularly inspect the griddle for any signs of rust. If rust appears, it should be addressed immediately to prevent further damage. Use a griddle stone or sandpaper to remove the rust, clean the area thoroughly, and reapply oil to re-season.

Deep Cleaning (Periodic Maintenance)

- **Heating for Cleaning**: Heat the griddle to a high temperature every few months or as needed. This process will help burn off stuck-on food particles and grease, making it easier to scrape and clean.
- **Use a Griddle Cleaner**: For a deeper clean, use a commercial griddle cleaner following the manufacturer's instructions. These cleaners can help remove stubborn residues and provide a thorough cleaning.
- **Rinse and Dry:** After using any cleaning agents, rinse the surface with clean water and dry it thoroughly to avoid chemical buildup or rusting.

- **Seasoning**: After deep cleaning, it's crucial to season the surface again to restore its non-stick properties. Heat the griddle, apply a thin layer of oil, and let it burn until it stops smoking. Repeat this process several times.

Storage Tips

- **Cover the Griddle**: Always cover your Blackstone griddle with a suitable cover when not in use. This protects it from the elements and keeps it clean.
- **Store in a Dry Place**: If possible, store your griddle in a dry, covered area to prevent exposure to moisture, which can lead to rust.

Following these daily cleaning and maintenance steps, you can keep your Blackstone griddle in top condition, ensuring it's always ready for your next cooking adventure. Regular care not only extends the life of your griddle but also ensures that it remains safe and enjoyable to use.

Even with diligent care, your Blackstone griddle may encounter some common cleaning challenges. Here's how to effectively troubleshoot and resolve these issues, keeping your griddle in pristine condition and ready for your next cooking session.

1. Sticky Residue

Problem: A sticky residue remains on the griddle surface after cooking and cleaning.

Solution:

- Heat the Griddle: Turn your griddle on and let it heat up. This can help loosen the sticky residue.
- Scrape Off: Remove the residue using a metal scraper once the griddle is hot.
- Clean and Season: After scraping, let the griddle cool, then clean it with a cloth dipped in hot water and a mild detergent. Rinse thoroughly with water, dry it, and apply a thin layer of cooking oil to re-season.

2. Rust Formation

Problem: Signs of rust appear on the griddle surface, especially after storage or exposure to moisture.

Solution:

- Remove Rust: When the griddle is dry, gently scrub the rust off with a griddle stone or fine steel wool.
- Clean the Area: After removing the rust, clean the area with a damp cloth to remove any metal particles.
- Re-season: Heat the griddle to open the metal's pores, apply a high smoke point oil, and let it burn off to re-season the surface. Repeat the oiling and heating a few times to build a protective layer.

3. Burnt-on Food

Problem: Food has burnt onto the griddle surface and is difficult to remove.

Solution:

- Soak the Area: If the food is stubbornly stuck, pour water over it and let it sit while the griddle is still warm. The steam will help loosen the food.
- Scrape and Scrub: Use a scraper to remove the food debris, then, if necessary, follow up with a griddle cleaning brick or scouring pad.
- Regular Maintenance: Clean the griddle regularly after each use to prevent food from building up and making it harder to clean.

4. Uneven Seasoning

Problem: The griddle surface has an uneven, patchy seasoning layer.

Solution:

- Clean the Surface: Clean the griddle thoroughly to remove any excess oil or food particles.
- Re-season Evenly: Apply a fresh layer of oil evenly across the entire surface. Heat the griddle until it smokes, and the oil burns off. Repeat several times to build a uniform seasoning layer.

5. Grease Buildup in Catch Tray

Problem: Excessive grease buildup in the grease catch tray, causing overflow or foul odors.

Solution:

- Regular Cleaning: Empty and clean the grease catch tray after every cooking session. Use hot, soapy water to remove all grease, rinse well, and dry before replacing.
- Use Liners: Consider using disposable liners or aluminum foil to line the tray, making cleanup quicker and easier.

6. Smoke and Odor During Cooking

Problem: Excessive smoke or unpleasant odors during cooking, even when the griddle is clean.

Solution:

- Check Food and Oil: Ensure you're using fresh oil and ingredients. Old or rancid oils and spoiled foods can cause bad smells and smoke.
- Proper Ventilation: Always use the griddle in a well-ventilated area. Lower the cooking temperature to reduce oil and food burning if smoke persists.

Addressing these common cleaning challenges with the appropriate solutions can maintain your Blackstone griddle's performance and longevity. Regular maintenance keeps your griddle ready for use and ensures that your cooking environment remains safe and enjoyable.

Direct vs. Indirect Cooking: Mastering the Heat

Understanding the nuances of direct and indirect cooking on your Blackstone griddle can significantly elevate your outdoor cooking game. These techniques, each suited for different dishes, allow you to utilize your griddle more effectively and diversify the range of meals you can prepare. Here's a deeper look into mastering these essential cooking methods.

Direct Cooking

Direct cooking on the Blackstone griddle is akin to traditional grilling, where food is cooked directly over the heat source. This method is perfect for foods that cook relatively quickly, require high heat, and benefit from searing to lock in flavors and juices.

- **Ideal Foods for Direct Cooking**: The direct method is best for cooking items like burgers, pancakes, bacon, eggs, and thin cuts of meat. This method benefits from consistent, high heat that sears the surface quickly, creating a delicious crust.
- **Technique**: To cook directly, preheat your griddle to a medium-high to high temperature before adding your food. The aim is to hear that sizzle when your food touches the griddle, indicating that the surface is hot enough to start the searing process.
- **Managing Hot Spots**: Blackstone griddles are designed for even heat distribution, but like any cooking surface, there can be slightly hotter areas. Use these to your advantage by searing meats on the hottest part of the griddle and moving them to a cooler section if they need additional time to cook through without burning.

Indirect Cooking

Indirect cooking is a method where food is cooked away from the direct heat source, allowing it to cook slower and typically at a lower temperature. This method is ideal for cooking thicker cuts of meat or dishes that require gentle, prolonged heat to reach the perfect doneness without charring the exterior.

- **Ideal Foods for Indirect Cooking**: Foods that benefit from slow cooking, such as thick steaks, whole vegetables like corn on the cob, or even delicate fish fillets, are perfect for indirect cooking. This method is also excellent for items that might burn if exposed to high heat for an extended period.
- **Technique**: Indirect cooking can be simulated on a Blackstone griddle by using low heat settings and utilizing the griddle's surface area. After searing your food over direct heat, move it to a cooler part of the griddle. If your model has multiple burners, turn off one burner or set it to low to create a cooler zone.
- **Covering the Food**: A dome or basting cover can enhance indirect cooking on a griddle by trapping heat around the food, mimicking an oven-like environment. This is particularly useful for ensuring thicker items are cooked through without the outside becoming overly done.

Combining Techniques

For the best results, many dishes benefit from a combination of both direct and indirect cooking methods:

- **Start with a Sear**: Sear meats or vegetables over direct heat to develop flavors and an appetizing crust.
- **Finish with Indirect Heat**: Move the food to a cooler part of the griddle to finish cooking. This technique is essential for thicker cuts of meat, ensuring that the inside reaches the desired level of doneness without the outside burning.

Advanced Tips

- **Preheating**: Always allow your griddle to preheat thoroughly. An adequately heated griddle ensures optimal cooking using direct or indirect methods.
- **Temperature Zones**: Experiment with creating different temperature zones on your griddle for more versatile cooking options. This can be particularly useful when preparing dishes requiring different cooking temperatures.

Temperature Control and Cooking Times

Effective temperature control and proper cooking times are essential for perfectly cooked meals on your Blackstone griddle. Understanding how to manage the heat and the cooking duration can make the difference between mediocre and mouth-watering dishes. This section will guide you through the basics of temperature management and provide general cooking times for various common griddle foods.

Temperature Control on the Blackstone Griddle
The Blackstone griddle offers a broad range of temperature settings, allowing you to cook various dishes perfectly. Here's how to master temperature control:

1. Know Your Zones
- **High Heat (400-450°F)**: Ideal for searing meats such as steaks and burgers, high heat develops a flavorful crust quickly. This temperature range is also perfect for stir-frying vegetables.
- **Medium Heat (300-375°F)**: Best for cooking chicken, seafood, and pancakes. It provides enough heat to cook thoroughly without burning delicate items.
- **Low Heat (200-250°F)**: Suitable for simmering sauces, cooking eggs, or keeping food warm without overcooking.

2. Preheating the Griddle
Always preheat your griddle for 10-15 minutes, regardless of what you are cooking. A properly preheated surface ensures foods start cooking immediately upon contact, crucial for achieving a good sear and preventing sticking.

3. Using a Thermometer
For precise cooking, especially when preparing thick cuts of meat, use an infrared thermometer to check the surface temperature of your griddle. This tool can help you maintain the exact heat needed for different cooking phases.

General Cooking Times for Common Foods
Below are some general guidelines for cooking times and temperatures for various foods on the Blackstone griddle. Remember, these approximations can vary based on specific factors such as food thickness and external temperatures.

Steaks
- High Heat: Sear for 2-3 minutes per side.
- Medium Heat: Cook to desired doneness, usually 4-8 minutes per side, depending on thickness.

Burgers
- Medium-High Heat: Cook for 4-5 minutes per side for medium-rare.

Chicken Breasts
- Medium Heat: Cook 6-8 minutes per side until the internal temperature reaches 165°F.

Fish Fillets
- Medium Heat: Cook for 3-4 minutes per side, depending on thickness.

Vegetables
- Medium-High Heat: Cooking times vary widely; for example, bell peppers take 3-4 minutes per side, while denser vegetables like carrots might take longer.

Eggs
- Low Heat: Cook scrambled eggs for 3-5 minutes, stirring frequently. For fried eggs, cook for 2-3 minutes per side for over-easy.

Pancakes
- Medium Heat: Cook for 2-3 minutes per side until bubbles form and the edges begin to set.

Tips for Consistent Results
- **Monitor and Adjust**: Always monitor the food as it cooks and adjust the temperature if necessary. If food is cooking too quickly and starting to burn, reduce the heat.
- **Rest Your Meats**: Allow meats to rest for a few minutes off the griddle before serving to let the juices redistribute.
- **Experiment**: Don't be afraid to adjust times and temperatures based on your experiences. Each Blackstone griddle can perform slightly differently, especially in various environmental conditions.

Mastering the art of temperature control and timing on your Blackstone griddle will enhance your cooking and ensure delicious results with every meal. As you become more familiar with your griddle, you'll find it easier to tweak and perfect your cooking methods.

Ensuring Food Safety: Hygiene and Handling

Maintaining high hygiene standards and proper handling techniques is crucial when using your Blackstone griddle. Food safety is essential to prevent foodborne illnesses and ensure that your meal is delicious and safe. Here's a comprehensive guide to help you uphold food safety standards while cooking on your griddle.

1. Proper Cleaning and Maintenance
Pre-Cleaning Steps
- **Clean Before First Use**: Before you start cooking on your Blackstone griddle for the first time, wash the cooking surface with warm, soapy water. Rinse thoroughly and dry completely. This initial cleaning removes any manufacturing residues or dust.
- **Regular Cleaning**: After each use, let the griddle cool down slightly, then scrape off food particles with a griddle scraper. Wipe the surface with a paper towel or a cloth soaked in warm, soapy water. Rinse with clean water and dry thoroughly.

Deep Cleaning
- **Scrubbing the Surface**: For a deeper clean, use a griddle-cleaning brick or pads designed for metal surfaces. Scrub gently to remove stubborn residues without damaging the seasoning.

- **Seasoning After Cleaning**: After thorough cleaning, reapply a thin layer of oil to the griddle surface and heat it to re-season. This step helps maintain the non-stick surface and prevents rust.

2. Handling Raw Foods Safely
Separate Raw from Cooked
- **Use Separate Utensils and Plates**: Always use separate cutting boards, utensils, and plates for raw and cooked foods. This prevents cross-contamination, which is crucial for food safety.
- **Storage**: Store raw meats, poultry, and seafood on the bottom shelf of your refrigerator to prevent their juices from contaminating other foods. Use airtight containers to keep them fresh.

Thawing Meat Properly
- **Safe Thawing Methods**: Thaw frozen meats in the refrigerator, cold water, or microwave. Never thaw food at room temperature, as this can promote bacterial growth.

3. Cooking Temperatures and Times
Know Your Targets
- **Use a Food Thermometer**: Always check the internal temperature of your food with a reliable thermometer. This ensures that meat, poultry, and seafood are cooked to a safe temperature:
  - Poultry: 165°F (74°C)
  - Ground Meat: 160°F (71°C)
  - Steaks and Chops: 145°F (63°C) with a rest time of at least 3 minutes
  - Fish: 145°F (63°C)

Consistent Cooking
- **Preheat Properly**: Ensure your griddle is preheated to the recommended temperature before adding food. This helps achieve a good sear and cooks food evenly.
- **Avoid Overcrowding**: Give your food enough space on the griddle to cook thoroughly. Overcrowding can lower the temperature and lead to uneven cooking.

4. Cross-Contamination Prevention
Clean Surfaces and Tools
- **Sanitize Frequently**: Wash your hands, griddle tools, and surfaces with hot, soapy water before and after handling raw foods. For added safety, sanitize them with one tablespoon of chlorine bleach per gallon of water.
- **Use Disposable Gloves**: Consider using disposable gloves when handling raw meats or seafood. Change gloves frequently to prevent contamination.

Safe Food Storage
- **Refrigerate Promptly**: Refrigerate leftovers within two hours of cooking. Use shallow containers to cool food quickly and evenly. Label leftovers with the date to keep track of their freshness.

5. General Food Handling Tips
Hand Hygiene
- **Wash Hands Frequently**: Wash your hands with soap and warm water for at least 20 seconds before and after handling food, using the restroom, and touching any potentially contaminated surfaces.
- **Use Paper Towels**: Use paper towels to handle raw foods and clean surfaces. Dispose of them immediately after use to avoid contamination.

Monitoring and Adjusting
- **Stay Attentive**: Watch your food while cooking to avoid overcooking or undercooking. Adjust the temperature as needed to maintain safe cooking conditions.

By adhering to these hygiene and handling guidelines, you can confidently enjoy cooking on your Blackstone griddle, knowing that you're serving safe, delicious meals every time. Remember, a little extra care in food safety practices goes a long way in ensuring a healthy and enjoyable dining experience.

Meat Mastery on the Griddle

Types of Meats and Best Cuts
Griddling meat is an art that combines the right cuts with the perfect griddle techniques. The Blackstone griddle's expansive cooking surface offers a superb platform for cooking various types of meat, from succulent steaks to perfect patties. Understanding the types of meats and the best cuts suitable for griddling will elevate your cooking skills and help you impress at your next cookout.

Beef: Rich Flavors and Versatility

Beef is a favorite for its rich flavor and versatility. Here are some top cuts for griddling:

- **Ribeye Steak**: Known for its marbling, ribeye is ideal for griddling due to its fat content, which provides flavor and keeps the meat moist during cooking.
- **Sirloin Steak**: A leaner option than ribeye, sirloin offers a good balance of flavor and tenderness without too much fat.
- **Ground Beef**: Perfect for burgers, ground beef should have a fat content of around 15-20% to ensure juicy, flavorful patties that don't dry out on the griddle.

Pork: Delightfully Different Textures

Pork offers a range of cuts that can transform into tender, flavorful dishes when cooked on a griddle:

- **Pork Chops**: For the best flavor, choose bone-in pork chops. The bone helps distribute heat evenly, preventing the meat from drying out.
- **Bacon**: Nothing griddles like bacon. Its high-fat content renders slowly, crisping up beautifully without burning.
- **Sausages**: Slowly griddle sausages to cook them evenly inside and out, achieving a perfect snap with every bite.

Chicken: A Lighter Choice

Chicken is a go-to protein for many because it's lean and cooks quickly:

- **Chicken Breasts**: Pound chicken breasts to an even thickness before griddling to ensure they cook evenly.
- **Chicken Thighs**: These are more forgiving than breasts due to their higher fat content, making them juicier and more complicated to overcook.
- **Ground Chicken**: Excellent for making chicken burgers or griddle meatballs, ground chicken should be seasoned well as it is naturally lean.

Seafood: Fast Cooking and Flavorful

Seafood cooks quickly and benefits from the consistent heat of a griddle:

- **Shrimp**: Whether skewered or grilled directly on the griddle, shrimp cook in just a few minutes and are incredibly versatile.
- **Scallops**: With a high heat for a short time, scallops develop a gorgeous crust with a tender, succulent interior.
- **Fish Fillets**: Choose firm fish like salmon or halibut for griddling. Lighter, flakier fish may break apart but can be cooked effectively with a griddle-friendly fish basket.

Game Meats: An Exotic Alternative

For those looking to try something different, game meats offer unique flavors and textures:

Venison: Steaks and burgers from deer are lean and rich in flavor.

They should be cooked quickly over high heat to medium-rare to avoid toughening.

- **Bison**: Similar to beef but leaner, bison steaks and burgers offer a sweet, rich flavor ideal for the high heat of a griddle.

Selecting and Storing Premium Meat

Selecting premium cuts and proper storage are crucial steps to ensure that every meal you prepare is delicious and safe. Here's a guide to help you choose the best meat for griddling and tips on storing it effectively.

Selecting Premium Meat

1. Understanding Meat Quality Grades

The USDA graded beef quality in the United States, with grades like Prime, Choice, and Select. Prime grade denotes the highest quality, featuring abundant marbling, key to flavor and tenderness. For pork and poultry, look for terms like "air-chilled" or "organic," indicating higher quality and better handling practices.

2. Examining the Meat

- **Color and Texture**: Fresh beef should be bright red and firm to the touch. Pork should be pale pink with a fine grain, and chicken should be pinkish without any gray tones.
- **Marbling**: Good marbling (fat distributed throughout the muscle) is a sign of quality for beef and lamb as it enhances flavor and juiciness.
- **Smell**: Good meat should not have an off or strong odor. A fresh, mild smell is indicative of quality and freshness.

3. Buying from Trusted Sources

Buy meat from reputable butchers or stores known for quality. Trusted sources handle meat properly, ensuring freshness and providing detailed information about its origin and characteristics.

Storing Meat Properly

1. Refrigeration

- **Short-Term Storage**: Store meat in your fridge's coldest part and use it within a few days of purchase. Beef lasts longer than poultry or pork.
- **Packaging**: If not used immediately, please wrap the meat in plastic wrap or place it in an airtight container to prevent air exposure, which can lead to spoilage.

2. Freezing

- **Preparation for Freezing**: For long-term storage, freeze meat tightly wrapped in heavy-duty aluminum foil, freezer wrap, or in a heavy-duty freezer bag to prevent freezer burn.
- **Labeling**: Always label your frozen meat with the date of freezing. This helps manage storage and ensures you use the oldest stocks first.
- **Thawing**: Thaw frozen meat in the fridge or in cold water, changing the water every 30 minutes for safety. Avoid room temperature thawing to prevent bacterial growth.

BEEF CUTS

TOP LOIN STEAK BONELESS	TENDERLOIN ROAST	TENDERLOIN STEAK
TOP LOIN STEAK BONE-IN	T-BONE STEAK	PORTERHOUSE STEAK

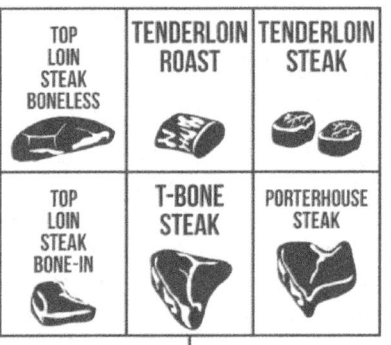

RIBEYE STEAK BONELESS	BACK RIBS
RIBEYE ROAST BONELESS	RIB STEAK	RIB ROAST

TOP SIRLOIN STEAK BONELESS	TRI-TIP STEAK	TRI-TIP ROAST

EYE ROUND STEAK	EYE ROUND ROAST	ROUND TIP ROAST
BOTTOM ROUND ROAST	TOP ROUND STEAK	BOTTOM ROUND STEAK WESTERN GRILLER
ROUND TIP STEAK	SIRLOIN TIP CENTER ROAST	SIRLOIN TIP CENTER STEAK
	SIRLOIN TIP SIDE STEAK	

ROUND   SIRLOIN   SHORT LOIN   **RIB**   **CHUCK**

FLANK   SHORT PLATE   FORE SHUNK   BRISKET

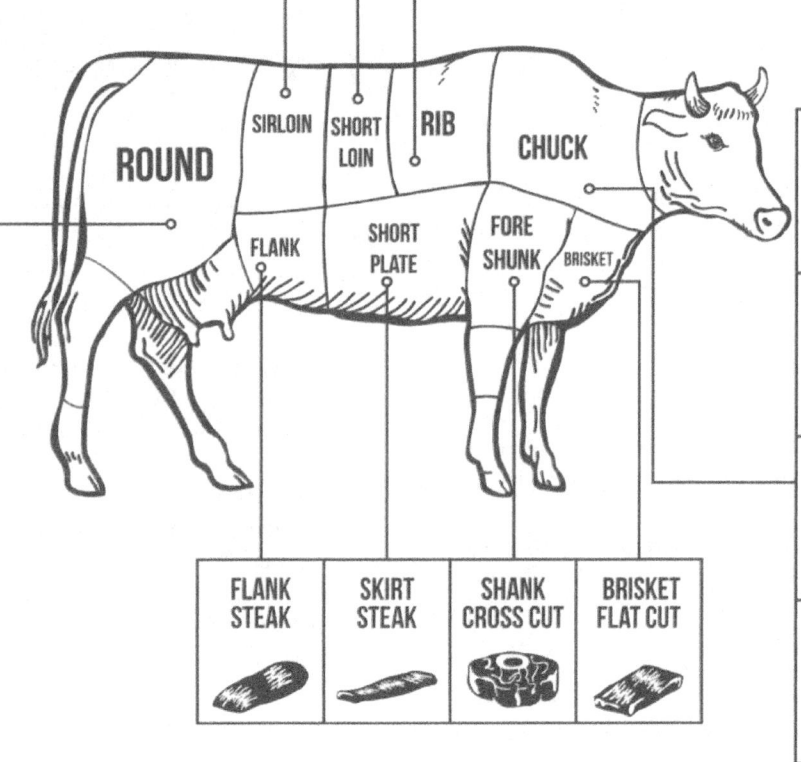

FLANK STEAK	SKIRT STEAK	SHANK CROSS CUT	BRISKET FLAT CUT

BONELESS SHORT RIBS	SHOULDER PETITE TENDER MEDALLIONS	SHOULDER PETITE TENDER
SHOULDER POT ROAST BONELESS	SHOULDER STEAK BONELESS	SHOULDER CENTER RANCH STEAK
CHUCK EYE STEAK BONELESS	SHOULDER TOP BLADE STEAK	SHOULDER TOP BLADE STEAK FLAT IRON
CHUCK STEAK BONELESS	CHUCK BONE 7 POT ROAST	CHUCK BONELESS POT ROAST

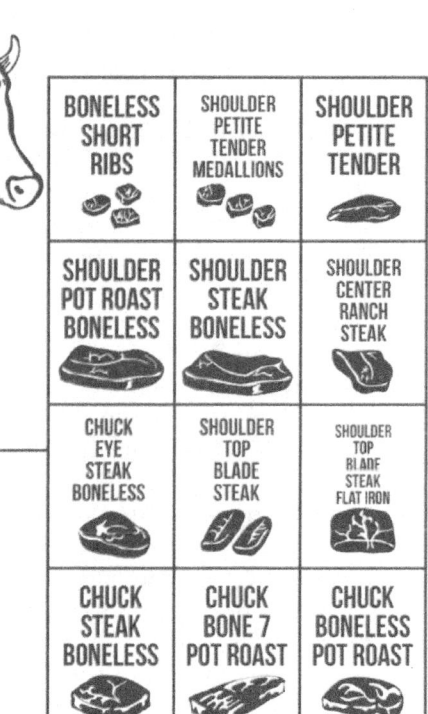

Perfect Steak on Your Blackstone Griddle

Grilling the perfect steak on your Blackstone Griddle is an art that combines technique with a bit of science. As the weather warms up, it's the perfect time to master this skill. Grilling the perfect steak on your Blackstone Griddle is an art that combines technique with a bit of science. As the weather warms up, it's the perfect time to master this skill.

1. Selecting the Right Steak
Choosing the right steak is crucial. Ribeye, known for its marbling, provides a great balance of flavor and tenderness due to its fat content. A good steak should be thick—about two fingers wide—to ensure it cooks evenly and remains juicy. If Ribeye isn't your preference, New York strips, fillets, or sirloins are also excellent choices. Look for steaks with good marbling and a thick cut for the best results.

2. Preparing Your Steak
Before you grill, preparation is key:
- **Dry Your Steak**: Pat the steak dry to remove any excess moisture. This step is essential for achieving a perfect sear.
- **Salting**: Apply about a quarter teaspoon of salt per pound of steak, not forgetting the sides. Salt draws out moisture, bringing it to the surface, where it can then reabsorb or evaporate, concentrating the steak's flavor. For an enhanced taste, you can salt your steak 24 hours in advance and refrigerate it.

3. Preheating Your Griddle
Heat your Blackstone Griddle to between 450°F and 550°F. A properly heated griddle is essential for creating that delicious crust through the Maillard reaction—a chemical reaction between amino acids and reducing sugars that gives browned food its distinctive flavor.

4. Cooking Techniques
- **Apply Oil**: Right before cooking, add a light coat of a high-smoke point oil, like an avocado or olive oil blend. This helps prevent sticking and adds to the flavor.
- **Searing the Steak**: Place the steak on the griddle and listen for that satisfying sizzle. After about a minute, flip the steak to prevent overcooking on one side and continue flipping every minute to ensure even cooking.
- **Two-Zone Cooking Method**: Utilize different heat zones on your griddle. Sear the steak on the hotter part to lock in flavors and move it to a cooler part to finish cooking. This technique allows for better control over the cooking temperature, ensuring your steak doesn't overcook.

5. Adding Flavor and Finishing Touches
Once your steak reaches the desired internal temperature (130°F for medium-rare), consider finishing it with a butter baste:
- **Prepare a Butter Bath**: On the griddle, melt some butter along with herbs like rosemary and thyme, and garlic to infuse the butter with flavor.
- **Baste the Steak**: Spoon this flavorful butter over the steak as it finishes cooking, adding richness and depth to its flavor.

6. Resting Your Steak
Always let your steak rest for about five minutes after cooking. Resting allows the juices to redistribute throughout the meat, ensuring a juicy, flavorful steak.

7. Serving Your Masterpiece
Serve your steak with the butter herb sauce from the griddle. Drizzle it over the meat to enhance its flavor. The combination of the seasoned, perfectly cooked steak with the aromatic butter sauce will impress any guest.

Tips and Tricks
- **Always start with a preheated griddle** to ensure a good sear.
- **Use an infrared thermometer** to check your griddle's temperature for precise cooking.
- **Experiment with different seasonings and marinades** to find your perfect steak flavor.
- **Keep flipping to a minimum**; turning the steak once or twice is enough to achieve an even cook without losing moisture.

Mastering the Art of Smash Burgers on Your Blackstone Griddle

Grilling the perfect smash burger on your Blackstone Griddle can transform your cookouts into an eagerly awaited event. Smash burgers, known for their crispy edges and juicy centers, are a fan favorite. This chapter will guide you through each step to achieve smash burger perfection, from preparation to the final delicious product.

1. Selecting and Preparing Your Ingredients
- **Choosing the Right Meat**: For optimal flavor and texture, use high-quality ground beef with a fat content of about 20% (80/20). This ratio ensures juicy, flavorful burgers after cooking.
- **Forming the Patties**: Rather than forming tightly packed, pre-shaped patties, loosely roll your ground beef into balls. This helps in creating that iconic smash burger texture. For standard burgers, aim for balls about 4-5 ounces in weight. Smaller sizes, like 2-3 ounces, are ideal if you're planning sliders or stacked burgers.
- **Seasoning**: Liberal seasoning is crucial. Salt the meatballs just before placing them on the griddle. Salt enhances flavor and helps extract proteins from the surface, which aids in forming a delicious crust.

2. Cooking the Smash Burgers
- **Preheat Your Griddle**: Heat your Blackstone Griddle to a medium-high setting. A well-heated griddle is essential for creating that crave-worthy crust.

- **The Smash Technique**: Place a ball of meat on the griddle, then firmly press down with a burger press or heavy spatula, using parchment paper to prevent sticking. Smash the burger until it's thin, which increases its surface area for a better Maillard reaction (flavorful browning). Hold the press for about 10 seconds to ensure good contact with the hot surface.
- **Cooking**: Allow the burger to cook undisturbed until the edges brown and the top begins to seep juices. This usually takes about 1-2 minutes. Flip the burger, add cheese, and cover with a bun top to steam the bun and melt the cheese simultaneously.
- **Assembling the Burgers**: After the cheese has melted and the burger is cooked to your liking, stack it on the bun bottom, which has been prepped by placing the heel on top under the burger as it cooks. This technique keeps the buns warm and ready to absorb delicious juices.

3. Additional Tips
- **Use High-Quality Fats**: If your beef is leaner, consider adding a small amount of high-quality fat like duck fat or clarified butter (ghee) to the griddle before adding your meat. This enhances flavor and aids in the cooking process without burning.
- **Bun Preparation**: For an extra touch of flavor, brush your buns with mayonnaise and lightly toast them on the griddle before assembling your burgers.
- **Resting**: Allow the cooked burgers to rest for a minute or two before serving. This helps the juices redistribute throughout the meat, ensuring each bite is moist and flavorful.

Following these steps, you canserve up delicious smash burgers at your next gathering, complete with a custom burger sauce that will impress you. Preparation and heat management are the keys to great smash burgers on your Blackstone Griddle. With a little practice, you'll be a smash burger master in no time!

Creative Griddle Tricks: Elevating Your Outdoor Cooking Game

I'm thrilled to share five ingenious griddle tricks that will elevate your outdoor cooking game. Whether you're looking to perfect your breakfast, host a fish fry, or add a dramatic flair to your gatherings, these tips are for you.

1. Mason Jar Egg Ring for Perfect Breakfast Sandwiches
Don't have a traditional egg ring? No problem! A mason jar lid can be an excellent substitute for crafting the perfect egg for your breakfast sandwiches. Here's how:

- **Prep**: Lightly spray the mason jar lid and place it on the griddle.
- **Cook**: Crack an egg into the lid, add a splash of water around it, and cover with a dome to steam. This method ensures your egg cooks evenly without burning the bottom, giving it that desirable, fast-food-style appearance.

2. Deep Frying on the Griddle
Believe it or not, your griddle can double as a deep fryer. Use a foil pan instead of a cast iron skillet for efficient heating, as it heats up faster. Here's the step-by-step:

- **Setup**: Place a foil pan on the griddle and fill it with oil (peanut oil is an excellent choice for its high smoke point).
- **Heat**: Start heating when you turn on the griddle, aiming for an oil temperature of about 350°F. This setup is perfect for cooking anything from tortilla chips for nachos to crispy chicken wings.

3. Turning Your Griddle into an Oven
Your griddle can mimic an oven's functionality with just a dome and a small wire rack. This setup is perfect for baking items like biscuits or cinnamon rolls outdoors.

- **Method**: Place the food item on the wire rack and cover it with the dome. The enclosed space circulates heat like an oven, allowing you to bake without direct contact with the griddle's surface and preventing the bottoms from burning.

4. The Volcano Onion Trick
A famous showstopper at Hibachi restaurants, the volcano onion is easy to recreate on your griddle.

- **Prepare**: Cut an onion into thick slices and build a tower-shaped structure using the middle parts.
- **Cook**: Place the onion layers on the griddle, add a high-proof alcohol like rum, and ignite to create the dramatic "volcano" effect. This not only entertains but also adds a grilled flavor to the onions.

5. Griddle Popcorn: A Fun Family Activity
Making popcorn on your griddle is possible and a delightful way to engage with your family.

- **Prepare**: Spread oil on the griddle and heat it up. Add popcorn kernels and cover them with a dome to concentrate the heat.
- **Cook**: Shake the dome occasionally to prevent the kernels from burning. Once the popping slows down, your fresh popcorn is ready to enjoy with your favorite seasonings.

These griddle tricks not only enhance the versatility of your cooking equipment but also add an element of fun and creativity to your culinary endeavors. Each method opens up new possibilities for meals and snacks that go beyond traditional griddling. So next time you fire up your griddle, try these tricks and impress your family and friends with your innovative cooking skills.

10 Essential Griddle Tips for Perfect Outdoor Cooking

Griddling isn't just a way to cook food; it's an art form that blends technique with timing to achieve culinary perfection. Whether new to griddling or looking to refine your skills, these ten essential tips will help you master the griddle and impress with every meal.

1. Mastering Sunny-Side-Up Eggs

Are you struggling with burnt bottoms on your sunny-side-up eggs? The secret is in the steam. Set your griddle to a lower temperature, crack the eggs onto the griddle, add a splash of water around the eggs, and quickly cover them with a dome or lid. The steam will cook the tops of the eggs without overcooking the bottoms.

2. Monitoring Griddle Temperature

Griddles can get extremely hot, so managing the temperature is crucial. Use an infrared thermometer to ensure you cook at optimal heat, especially when transitioning from restaurant equipment to a residential griddle. This will prevent food from burning and ensure even cooking.

3. Choosing the Right Tools

You can invest in a good-quality spatula or a dough scraper with a beveled edge. This tool is essential for efficiently lifting foods like smash burgers off the griddle while preserving their delicious crust.

4. Utilizing a Warming Rack

A warming rack is invaluable for managing cooking space and keeping prepared foods at an ideal temperature. It's particularly useful when some meal components are ready before others.

5. Toasting Bread with Mayonnaise

Instead of butter, try toasting your bread with mayonnaise. The oil and egg in the mayonnaise create a beautifully crisp and flavorful crust that's hard to achieve with butter alone. Whether you're making a grilled cheese or a BLT, mayonnaise can transform your toasted bread.

6. The Cheese Steak Flip

For an easy way to assemble a cheesesteak or any sandwich with toppings like sauce, peppers, and onions, place the cheese on the cooked ingredients, add a splash of water for steam, and then top with the bun. You can slide your spatula underneath and flip it directly into the bread for a perfect sandwich every time.

7. Optimal Placement for Toasting Bread

Use the cooler part of your griddle, often near the grease trap, to toast bread. This prevents the bread from toasting too quickly and burning, allowing for a golden, evenly toasted surface.

8. Doubling Up on Portions

When cooking on a large griddle, take advantage of the space by preparing extra portions. Cooking meals like fried rice or chicken in bulk ensures you have delicious leftovers for the week, saving time and energy on future meals.

9.Multipurpose Use of Steak Weights

While typically used for smash burgers, a steak weight or burger press is also excellent for achieving perfectly crispy hash browns or keeping bacon flat. At the same time, it cooks—experiment with using the weight on other foods that benefit from even direct contact with the griddle surface.

10. Understanding Cooking Order

To optimize your cooking process, start with the ingredients that take the longest to cook and end with those that cook the quickest. For breakfast, this might mean starting with meats, followed by potatoes, and finishing with eggs or vegetables.

With these ten tips, you'll enhance your griddling skills and enjoy more consistent and delicious results. Remember, griddling is as much about timing and technique as the food itself. Now, fire up that griddle and get cooking!

Pro Tips and FAQs

Whether you're a seasoned griddle master or a newcomer to outdoor cooking with a Blackstone griddle, you likely have questions about how to get the most out of your cooking experience. This chapter compiles expert answers to some of the most frequently asked questions about Blackstone griddles and professional tips to enhance your griddling skills.

Q1: How often should I season my Blackstone griddle?

A1: Seasoning your griddle is crucial for maintaining a non-stick surface and preventing rust. Initially, you should season your griddle thoroughly before the first use. After that, it's an excellent practice to lightly re-season the griddle after each use, especially after a deep clean. If you notice food starting to stick more than usual or after storing your griddle for an extended period, it's time for another thorough seasoning session.

Q2: Can I cook with pots and pans on my Blackstone griddle?

A2: Absolutely! One of the great features of the Blackstone griddle is its versatility. You can use pots and pans directly on the surface, like on a regular stove. This is particularly useful for heating sauces, cooking rice, or even boiling water, expanding your cooking options.

Q3: What is the best way to clean the griddle after cooking?

A3: Wait until the griddle cools down slightly but is still warm for daily cleaning. Scrape off any food particles with a metal scraper or spatula. Then, wipe the surface clean with a paper towel. For a deeper clean, use a cloth with warm, soapy water after scraping, rinse with clean water, and apply a thin layer of oil after drying. This helps maintain the seasoning and prevents rust.

Q4: How do I store my Blackstone griddle when not in use?

A4: Proper storage is critical to extending the life of your griddle. After ensuring the griddle is clean and completely dry, apply a light coat of cooking oil to the surface.
Use a griddle cover to protect it from the elements. Ideally, store the griddle in a dry, covered area to prevent exposure to moisture. If outdoor storage is unavoidable, ensure the cover is secure and check periodically for any signs of moisture or rust.

Q5: What types of oils are best for seasoning the Blackstone griddle?

A5: High-smoke point oils are ideal for seasoning because they can withstand high temperatures without breaking down. Some of the best seasoning oils include flaxseed, canola, vegetable, and shortening. These oils create a durable, non-stick surface on the griddle.

Q6: Can I leave my Blackstone griddle outside all year?

A6: While Blackstone griddles are durable, constant exposure to the elements can shorten their lifespan. If you need to leave your griddle outside, use a heavy-duty cover to protect it from rain, snow, and sunlight. However, store your griddle in a garage or shed during harsh weather, especially over winter.

Q7: What should I do if my griddle surface develops rust?

A7: If you spot rust, don't panic—it's usually fixable. Scrape off the rust with a metal scraper or sandpaper, then clean the area thoroughly. Re-season the surface by heating the griddle and applying a layer of cooking oil. Repeat the oiling and heating several times to rebuild the protective coating.

Q8: Are there any foods I shouldn't cook on the Blackstone griddle?

A8: Blackstone griddles are incredibly versatile, but very sugary foods like marinades and sauces can leave a sticky residue that is hard to clean. Additionally, acidic foods such as tomatoes should be cooked carefully, as they can damage the seasoning layer if left to cook for extended periods.

Q9: How can I prevent food from sticking to my Blackstone griddle?

A9: Preventing food from sticking is primarily about proper griddle maintenance and cooking techniques. Here's what you can do:

- Ensure Proper Seasoning: A well-seasoned griddle is the first defense against sticking. Apply oil after each cleaning to maintain the seasoning layer regularly.
- Preheat the Griddle: Always allow the griddle to fully preheat before adding food. A sufficiently hot griddle helps to create an initial sear that prevents sticking.
- Control Temperature: Avoid cooking on excessively high heat unless necessary for searing. Foods cooked at too high a temperature can stick and burn.
- Use Enough Fat: While the seasoned surface is non-stick, using oil or butter when cooking helps prevent food from sticking and adds flavor.

This chapter is designed to help beginners get comfortable with their new kitchen companion. We'll cover everything from setup to your first cook, ensuring your experience is as enjoyable and successful as possible.

1. Setting Up Your Blackstone Griddle

Before you begin cooking, it's important to set up your griddle properly to ensure safety and optimal cooking performance:

- **Location**: Place your griddle outdoors in a well-ventilated area, away from any flammable structures like wooden fences or overhead branches. Make sure the surface is level to avoid uneven cooking or oil pooling.
- **Assembly**: Follow the manufacturer's instructions carefully to assemble your griddle. Ensure all parts are fitted securely.
- **Safety Check**: Before igniting the griddle, check for any gas leaks, especially if it's propane-powered. Apply a soapy water solution to the connections and hoses. If bubbles form, there's a leak. Tighten the connections or replace any faulty parts as necessary.

2. Initial Cleaning and Seasoning

Your Blackstone Griddle will perform best with a proper initial seasoning, which also helps create a natural non-stick surface:

- **Cleaning**: Wipe down the griddle surface with warm, soapy water to remove any protective oils or residues from manufacturing. Rinse thoroughly with water and dry with a clean cloth.
- **Heating**: Turn on the griddle to high heat and allow it to heat until it changes color (dark brown or bronze), indicating it's ready for oiling.
- **Seasoning**: Use a high-smoke point oil like canola, vegetable, or flaxseed oil. Apply a thin, even layer across the surface using a paper towel held with tongs. The griddle will smoke, which is part of the seasoning process. Allow the oil to burn off until the smoking stops, then repeat this process 3-4 times to build up a good seasoning layer.

3. Your First Cooking Session

For your first cooking experience, choose something simple and forgiving. Here's how to cook the perfect beginner's meal on your Blackstone:

- **Ingredient Preparation**: Start with an easy recipe, such as grilled vegetables or simple chicken breasts. Prepare all your ingredients ahead of time—this means washing, cutting, and seasoning as needed.
- **Preheating**: Turn your griddle on medium heat for 10-15 minutes before cooking. This ensures that the surface is evenly heated.
- **Cooking**: Place your ingredients on the griddle. Use tools like spatulas or tongs to move them around. For foods like burgers or pancakes, wait until you see bubbles or the edges are done before flipping.

- **Monitoring Temperature**: Keep an eye on the heat. If things are cooking too quickly or burning, turn the heat down. Conversely, if they're cooking too slowly, you may need to increase the heat slightly.

4. Cleaning and Maintenance Post-Cooking

Proper maintenance after each use will extend the life of your griddle and keep it performing well:

- **Cool Down**: Allow the griddle to cool slightly after turning it off, but while it's still warm...
- **Scrape Off Residues**: Use a griddle scraper to remove food particles and residues.
- **Wipe Down**: Wipe the surface with a cloth or paper towel. If necessary, use a little water to help remove stubborn particles.
- **Oil the Surface**: Once clean and dry, apply a light coat of cooking oil to protect the surface and maintain the seasoning.

BREAKFAST RECIPES

Classic American Pancakes

- 1 ½ cups all-purpose flour
- 3 ½ teaspoons baking powder
- 1 tablespoon sugar
- 1 teaspoon salt
- 1 ¼ cups milk
- 1 egg
- 3 tablespoons melted butter
- Additional butter for greasing the griddle
- Maple syrup and fresh berries (for serving)

PREP. TIME: 10 min

COOKING TIME: 15 min

SERVES: 4

1. **Preheat your Blackstone griddle to 375°F** (190°C). This moderate temperature is ideal for cooking pancakes without burning them.
2. **Combine the dry ingredients**: Sift together the flour, baking powder, sugar, and salt in a large bowl.
3. **Mix the wet ingredients**: In another bowl, whisk together the milk, egg, and melted butter until well combined.
4. **Make the pancake batter**: Pour the wet ingredients into the dry ingredients. Stir using a wooden spoon until just combined. The batter should be slightly lumpy; do not overmix.
5. **Grease the griddle**: Lightly butter the preheated griddle. This will prevent the pancakes from sticking and give them a golden color.
6. **Cook the pancakes**: Pour ¼ cup of batter for each pancake onto the griddle. Cook for 2-3 minutes or until bubbles form on the surface and the edges appear set.
7. **Flip the pancakes**: Carefully flip each pancake using a spatula. Cook for 1-2 minutes on the other side or until golden brown is cooked through.
8. **Serve warm**: For a classic breakfast, serve the pancakes hot off the griddle with maple syrup and a side of fresh berries.

Southwestern Breakfast Burrito

- 8 large eggs
- 1/2 cup milk
- Salt and pepper, to taste
- 1 tablespoon olive oil
- 1/2 pound chorizo sausage, casing removed and crumbled
- 1 large onion, diced
- 1 red bell pepper, diced
- 1 green bell pepper, diced
- 1 cup cooked black beans, drained and rinsed
- 4 large flour tortillas
- 1 cup shredded cheddar cheese
- 1/2 cup fresh cilantro, chopped
- Salsa and sour cream, for serving

PREP. TIME: 15 min

COOKING TIME: 10 min

SERVES: 4

1. **Preheat your Blackstone griddle to 350°F** (175°C).
2. **Cook the chorizo**: Add olive oil to the griddle, then add the crumbled chorizo. Cook for 3-4 minutes until browned, then remove and set aside.
3. **Sauté vegetables**: In the same oil, sauté onion and bell peppers for 3-5 minutes until softened.
4. **Scramble the eggs**: Add the egg mixture to the griddle, allowing it to set slightly, then gently scramble until softly set, about 2-3 minutes.
5. **Combine ingredients**: Return the chorizo to the griddle, add black beans, and mix everything with the scrambled eggs.
6. **Assemble the burritos**: Warm the tortillas on the griddle, then distribute the egg mixture among them. Top with cheddar cheese and cilantro, and fold to enclose the fillings.
7. **Serve**: Optionally, crisp the burritos on the griddle, seam-side down. Serve with salsa and sour cream.

Griddle French Toast with Cinnamon Butter

PREP. TIME: 10 min

COOKING TIME: 10 min

SERVES: 4

For the French Toast:
- 8 slices of thick-cut bread (brioche or challah works well)
- 4 large eggs
- 1 cup whole milk

- 2 teaspoons vanilla extract
- 1/2 teaspoon ground cinnamon
- Pinch of salt
- Butter for greasing the griddle

For the Cinnamon Butter:
- 1/2 cup unsalted butter, softened
- 2 tablespoons powdered sugar
- 1 teaspoon ground cinnamon
- 1/2 teaspoon vanilla extract

1. **Make the Cinnamon Butter**: In a small bowl, combine softened butter, powdered sugar, ground cinnamon, and vanilla extract. Mix until smooth and set aside.
2. **Prepare the French Toast Batter**: In a large mixing bowl, whisk together eggs, milk, vanilla extract, cinnamon, and a pinch of salt.
3. **Preheat the Griddle**: Heat your Blackstone griddle to 350°F (175°C) and lightly butter the surface.
4. **Dip the Bread**: Soak each slice of bread in the egg mixture for about 30 seconds per side, ensuring they are well coated but not soggy.
5. **Cook the French Toast**: Place the soaked bread slices on the griddle and cook for about 3-4 minutes on each side, or until golden brown and slightly crispy.
6. **Serve**: Serve the French toast hot, topped with a dollop of cinnamon butter and, if desired, a drizzle of maple syrup.

Egg and Sausage Breakfast Tacos

PREP. TIME: 10 min

COOKING TIME: 10 min

SERVES: 4

- 8 large eggs
- 1/4 cup milk
- Salt and pepper, to taste
- 1 tablespoon olive oil
- 1/2 pound ground sausage

- 1 small onion, diced
- 1 bell pepper, diced (any color)
- 8 small corn or flour tortillas
- 1/2 cup shredded cheddar cheese
- Optional garnishes: sliced avocado, fresh cilantro, salsa, sour cream

1. **Preheat the Griddle**: Heat your Blackstone griddle to medium-high (about 350°F).
2. **Cook the Sausage**: Add olive oil to the griddle, then add the sausage, breaking it into smaller pieces as it cooks. Once browned, remove the sausage from the griddle and set aside.
3. **Sauté Vegetables**: Add diced onion and bell pepper in the same oil. Sauté for about 2-3 minutes until softened.
4. **Scramble the Eggs**: In a bowl, whisk together eggs, milk, salt, and pepper. Pour the mixture onto the griddle, using a spatula to scramble the eggs as they cook gently. Cook until the eggs are just set, about 3-4 minutes.
5. **Combine Ingredients**: Add the cooked sausage back to the griddle, mixing it into the scrambled eggs.
6. **Warm the Tortillas**: Place tortillas on the griddle for about 30 seconds on each side, just to warm them.
7. **Assemble the Tacos**: Spoon the egg and sausage mixture into the warm tortillas. Top with shredded cheddar cheese, and if desired, add slices of avocado, a sprinkle of cilantro, a dollop of salsa, and/or a spoonful of sour cream.

Smoky Ham and Hash Brown Omelette

PREP. TIME: 25 min

COOKING TIME: 15 min

SERVES: 2

- 2 cups dehydrated hash browns
- Hot water (for rehydrating hash browns)
- 1 tablespoon butter, plus extra for cooking
- 1/2 cup diced ham (preferably a smoky variety)
- 1/2 cup diced onion

- 1/2 cup sliced mushrooms
- 5 large eggs
- 2 tablespoons heavy whipping cream
- Salt and pepper, to taste
- 1/2 cup shredded cheddar cheese
- Optional: Additional oil for cooking

1. **Rehydrate Hash Browns**: Soak dehydrated hash browns in hot water for 20 minutes and drain well.
2. **Preheat the Griddle**: Set your Blackstone griddle to low heat (about 300°F).
3. **Sauté Fillings**: Melt butter on the griddle, then add ham, onions, and mushrooms. Cook until onions are translucent and ham is slightly browned.
4. **Prepare Eggs**: Whisk together eggs, heavy cream, salt, and pepper.
5. **Cook Hash Browns**: Spread hash browns evenly on the griddle, cooking until golden on both sides.
6. **Assemble Omelette**: Layer the sautéed fillings over the hash browns, pour the egg mixture over the top, and sprinkle with cheddar cheese.
7. **Cook Until Set**: Let the omelette cook undisturbed until the eggs set. Fold edges over the center with a spatula.
8. **Serve**: Once the bottom is crispy and golden, remove from heat, slice, and serve warm.

VEGETABLES AND SIDE DISHES

Portobello Mushroom Steak

- 4 large Portobello mushroom caps
- 1/4 cup olive oil
- 2 tablespoons balsamic vinegar
- 2 cloves garlic, minced
- 1 teaspoon soy sauce
- 1/2 teaspoon dried thyme
- Salt and freshly ground black pepper to taste
- Optional garnishes: Chopped parsley or fresh thyme

PREP. TIME: 15 min

COOKING TIME: 8 min

SERVES: 4

1. **Clean the Mushrooms**: Gently wipe the Portobello mushrooms with a damp cloth to clean. Remove the stems and scrape out the gills with a spoon.
2. **Prepare the Marinade**: In a small bowl, whisk together olive oil, balsamic vinegar, minced garlic, soy sauce, dried thyme, salt, and pepper.
3. **Marinate the Mushrooms**: Place the mushroom caps in a shallow dish or a large resealable plastic bag. Pour the marinade over the mushrooms, making sure they are well coated. Let them marinate for about 10 minutes, turning once halfway through.
4. **Preheat the Griddle**: Heat your Blackstone griddle to medium-high heat (around 375°F).
5. **Grill the Mushrooms**: Remove the mushrooms from the marinade, reserving any excess marinade for basting. Place the mushrooms cap-side down on the griddle. Grill for about 4 minutes on each side, basting occasionally with the reserved marinade until they are tender and have grill marks.
6. **Serve**: Transfer the grilled mushrooms to plates. Garnish with chopped parsley or fresh thyme for an extra touch of flavor.

Zucchini and Squash Ribbon Skewers

- 2 medium zucchini
- 2 medium yellow squash
- 2 tablespoons olive oil
- 1 teaspoon dried Italian herbs or herbes de Provence
- Salt and freshly ground black pepper to taste
- Optional: Lemon wedges for serving

PREP. TIME: 10 min

COOKING TIME: 10 min

SERVES: 4

1. **Prepare the Vegetables**: Use a vegetable peeler or a mandoline slicer to cut the zucchini and yellow squash into long, thin ribbons.
2. **Thread the Ribbons**: Carefully thread the zucchini and squash ribbons onto skewers, folding them in an accordion style to create a compact but visually appealing skewer.
3. **Season**: In a small bowl, mix together the olive oil, dried herbs, salt, and pepper. Brush this mixture over the skewered zucchini and squash ribbons, ensuring they are well coated on all sides.
4. **Preheat the Griddle**: Heat your Blackstone griddle to medium-high heat (about 375°F).
5. **Grill the Skewers**: Place the skewers on the hot griddle. Grill for about 4-5 minutes on each side or until the vegetables are tender and have charred grill marks.
6. **Serve**: Remove the skewers from the griddle and serve hot, with lemon wedges on the side for squeezing over the veggies if desired.

Smoky Grilled Tofu Tacos

PREP. TIME: 25 min
COOKING TIME: 10 min
SERVES: 4

- 14 oz firm tofu, pressed and drained
- 1/4 cup chipotle sauce
- 1 tablespoon soy sauce
- 1 tablespoon olive oil
- 1 teaspoon smoked paprika
- 1/2 teaspoon garlic powder
- Salt and pepper, to taste
- 8 small corn tortillas
- 1 ripe avocado, sliced
- 1/4 cup chopped fresh cilantro
- 2 limes, cut into wedges
- Optional garnishes: sliced radishes, diced tomatoes, and sliced red onions

1. **Marinate the Tofu**: Slice the tofu into 1/2-inch thick slabs. Whisk together the chipotle sauce, soy sauce, olive oil, smoked paprika, garlic powder, salt, and pepper in a shallow dish. Place the tofu slabs in the marinade, ensuring each piece is well coated. Let marinate for at least 15 minutes, turning once halfway through.
2. **Preheat the Griddle**: Heat your Blackstone griddle to medium-high heat (around 375°F).
3. **Grill the Tofu**: Remove the tofu from the marinade, letting excess drip off. Place the tofu on the hot griddle and grill for about 5 minutes per side or until the tofu is heated through and has nice grill marks.
4. **Warm the Tortillas**: While the tofu is grilling, place the corn tortillas on the griddle for about 30 seconds per side, just until they are warm and slightly charred. Wrap them in a clean cloth to keep them warm.
5. **Assemble the Tacos**: Slice the grilled tofu into thin strips. Place a few strips of tofu in each warm tortilla. Top with slices of avocado, a sprinkle of chopped cilantro, and optional garnishes like radishes, tomatoes, and onions.
6. **Serve**: Serve the tacos immediately with lime wedges on the side for squeezing over the top.

Grilled Sweet Potatoes with Lime and Cilantro

PREP. TIME: 10 min
COOKING TIME: 25 min
SERVES: 4

- 4 medium sweet potatoes
- 2 tablespoons olive oil
- Salt and pepper, to taste
- Zest of 2 limes
- 1/4 cup chopped fresh cilantro
- Additional lime wedges for serving

1. **Prepare the Sweet Potatoes**: Wash the sweet potatoes and cut them into wedges. Try to keep the wedges uniform in size to ensure even cooking.
2. **Preheat the Griddle**: Heat your Blackstone griddle to medium-high heat (around 375°F).
3. **Season the Wedges**: Place the sweet potato wedges in a large bowl. Drizzle with olive oil and season with salt and pepper. Toss to coat evenly.
4. **Grill the Sweet Potatoes**: Arrange the wedges on the hot griddle. Grill for about 12-15 minutes per side, turning occasionally, until they are golden and crispy on the outside and soft on the inside.
5. **Toss with Lime and Cilantro**: Transfer the grilled sweet potatoes back to the bowl once cooked. Add the lime zest and chopped cilantro, and toss everything together while the potatoes are still warm to enhance the flavors.
6. **Serve**: Serve the grilled sweet potatoes immediately, garnished with additional lime wedges for squeezing over the top.

Honey Black Pepper Brussels Sprouts

PREP. TIME: 10 min
COOKING TIME: 15 min
SERVES: 4

- 1 lb Brussels sprouts, halved
- 4 oz pancetta, diced
- 1/2 red onion, thinly sliced
- 2 tablespoons olive oil
- Salt and freshly ground black pepper to taste

For the Black Pepper Honey:
- 1/4 cup honey
- 1 teaspoon freshly ground black pepper
- 1 tablespoon chopped parsley

1. **Preheat the Griddle**: Heat your Blackstone griddle to medium heat (about 350°F).
2. **Cook the Pancetta**: Spread the diced pancetta on the griddle and cook until crispy, about 5-7 minutes. Once crisp, move the pancetta to a cooler part of the griddle.
3. **Sauté the Vegetables**: Add Brussels sprouts and sliced red onion to the rendered pancetta fat. Drizzle with olive oil, and season with salt and pepper. Cook for about 6 minutes, stirring occasionally, until the Brussels sprouts are tender and caramelized.
4. **Prepare the Black Pepper Honey**: While the vegetables cook, mix honey, black pepper, and chopped parsley in a small bowl until combined. This mixture should have a bold, peppery flavor balanced by the sweetness of the honey.
5. **Combine and Serve**: Bring the crispy pancetta back to the center of the griddle and mix with the sautéed Brussels sprouts and onions. Drizzle the black pepper honey over the vegetables directly on the griddle, tossing to coat evenly.
6. **Plate and Garnish**: Serve the Brussels sprouts family-style, garnished with additional parsley if desired. The honey mixture should give the sprouts a glossy, stained-glass appearance, enhancing both the flavor and presentation.

FISH AND SEAFOOD RECIPES

Grilled Lemon Garlic Shrimp Skewers

- 1 pound large shrimp, peeled and deveined
- 3 tablespoons olive oil
- Juice of 1 lemon, plus additional lemon wedges for serving
- 3 cloves garlic, minced
- 2 tablespoons fresh parsley, finely chopped
- Salt and freshly ground black pepper to taste

PREP. TIME: 15 min

COOKING TIME: 6 min

SERVES: 4

1. **Prepare the Marinade**: In a mixing bowl, combine olive oil, lemon juice, minced garlic, chopped parsley, salt, and pepper. Stir to mix well.
2. **Marinate the Shrimp**: Add the shrimp to the marinade and toss to ensure each shrimp is well coated. Cover and let marinate in the refrigerator for about 10 minutes.
3. **Preheat the Griddle**: Heat your Blackstone griddle to medium-high heat (around 375°F).
4. **Skewer the Shrimp**: Thread the marinated shrimp onto skewers. If using wooden skewers, make sure to soak them in water for at least 30 minutes beforehand to prevent burning.
5. **Grill the Shrimp**: Place the skewered shrimp on the hot griddle. Grill for about 3 minutes on each side or until the shrimp are pink, opaque, and slightly charred.
6. **Serve**: Remove the shrimp skewers from the griddle and serve immediately with additional lemon wedges for squeezing over the shrimp.

Crispy Fish and Chips

For the Fish:
- 4 large cod fillets, cut into pieces
- Salt and pepper, to taste
- 1 cup panko breadcrumbs
- 1/2 cup mayonnaise
- 1 tablespoon garlic paste

- 2 teaspoons Old Bay Seasoning, plus extra for fries
- Juice of half a lemon
- 2 tablespoons flat-leaf parsley, finely chopped
- Oil for shallow frying
- Butter for frying

For the Chips:
- 1 pound frozen Idaho fries
- Malt vinegar, for serving
- Ketchup, for serving
- Lemon wedges, for serving

PREP. TIME: 15 min

COOKING TIME: 10 min

SERVES: 4

1. **Prepare Dipping Sauce & Marinade**: In a mixing bowl, combine mayonnaise, garlic paste, 2 teaspoons Old Bay Seasoning, lemon juice, and chopped parsley. Mix well, taste, and adjust seasoning according to preference.
2. **Prepare the Fish**: Season the cod pieces with salt and pepper. Place the panko breadcrumbs on a tray. Brush each piece of fish with the mayonnaise mixture, then press into the breadcrumbs to coat thoroughly.
3. **Preheat the Blackstone**: Heat the Blackstone griddle to medium heat and add a mixture of butter and oil to prevent sticking.
4. **Cook the Chips**: If using the Blackstone air fryer drawer, place the fries in the drawer to cook. Alternatively, spread the fries on the griddle and cook until crispy, turning occasionally.
5. **Fry the Fish**: Add the breaded fish once the oil and butter are hot. Fry for 2-3 minutes per side or until golden brown is cooked through. Transfer to a cooling rack or a plate lined with paper towels to drain excess oil.
6. **Serve**: Arrange the crispy fish and chips on a platter. Sprinkle the fries with additional Old Bay Seasoning. Serve with malt vinegar, ketchup, and lemon wedges on the side.

Grilled Salmon with Dill Butter

PREP. TIME: 10 min
COOKING TIME: 10 min
SERVES: 4

- 4 salmon fillets, about 6 ounces each
- Salt and freshly ground black pepper, to taste
- Olive oil, for brushing

For the Dill Butter:
- 1/2 cup unsalted butter, softened
- 2 tablespoons fresh dill, finely chopped
- 1 teaspoon lemon zest
- 1 tablespoon lemon juice
- Salt, to taste

1. **Prepare the Dill Butter**: In a small bowl, mix the softened butter, chopped dill, lemon zest, and lemon juice together until well combined. Season with salt to taste. Place the mixture on a piece of plastic wrap or parchment paper and roll it into a log. Refrigerate until firm.
2. **Preheat the Griddle**: Heat your Blackstone griddle to medium-high heat (around 375°F).
3. **Prepare the Salmon**: Brush each salmon fillet lightly with olive oil and season both sides with salt and pepper.
4. **Grill the Salmon**: Place the salmon fillets on the griddle, skin side down, and grill for about 5 minutes. Carefully flip the fillets and cook for another 4-5 minutes until the salmon is cooked and flakes easily with a fork.
5. **Serve with Dill Butter**: Remove the salmon from the griddle and immediately top each fillet with a slice of the chilled dill butter. Allow the butter to melt slightly before serving.
6. **Garnish and Enjoy**: Serve the grilled salmon with a side of steamed vegetables or a fresh salad for a complete meal.

Grilled Scallops with Lemon Basil Sauce

PREP. TIME: 10 min
COOKING TIME: 6 min
SERVES: 4

- 16 large sea scallops, muscle removed
- Salt and freshly ground black pepper, to taste
- 2 tablespoons olive oil
- 2 tablespoons unsalted butter

For the Lemon Basil Sauce:
- 1/4 cup unsalted butter, melted
- Juice of 1 lemon
- 1/4 cup fresh basil leaves, finely chopped
- Salt, to taste

1. **Prepare the Scallops**: Pat the scallops dry with paper towels to ensure proper searing. Season both sides with salt and pepper, then lightly brush them with olive oil.
2. **Preheat the Griddle**: Heat your Blackstone griddle to medium-high heat (around 375°F).
3. **Grill the Scallops**: Place the scallops on the hot griddle and cook for about 3 minutes on each side or until they have a golden crust and are opaque throughout. Avoid moving them around too much to achieve a good sear.
4. **Make the Lemon Basil Sauce**: While the scallops are cooking, whisk together the melted butter, lemon juice, and chopped basil in a small bowl. Season with a pinch of salt to enhance the flavors.
5. **Serve**: Once the scallops are cooked, remove them from the griddle and immediately drizzle with the lemon basil sauce.
6. **Garnish and Enjoy**: Optionally, garnish with additional fresh basil leaves or lemon slices for an extra touch of freshness and visual appeal.

Spicy Grilled Calamari

PREP. TIME: 10 min
COOKING TIME: 4 min
SERVES: 4

- 1 pound calamari rings, cleaned
- 3 tablespoons olive oil
- 1 teaspoon crushed red pepper flakes (adjust to taste for spiciness)
- 2 cloves garlic, minced
- Zest of 1 lemon
- Salt, to taste
- Fresh parsley, chopped (for garnish)
- Lemon wedges for serving
- Marinara sauce or aioli, for dipping

1. **Prepare the Calamari**: In a large bowl, combine the calamari rings with olive oil, crushed red pepper flakes, minced garlic, and lemon zest. Toss well to ensure the calamari is evenly coated with the seasonings. Season with a pinch of salt.
2. **Preheat the Griddle**: Heat your Blackstone griddle to medium-high heat (around 375°F).
3. **Grill the Calamari**: Spread the seasoned calamari in a single layer on the hot griddle. Grill for about 2 minutes on each side or until the calamari is tender and slightly charred. Be careful not to overcook, as calamari can become rubbery if cooked too long.
4. **Serve**: Remove the calamari from the griddle and place on a serving platter. Garnish with chopped parsley and provide lemon wedges on the side for squeezing.
5. **Accompaniments**: Serve the spicy grilled calamari with your choice of marinara sauce or aioli for dipping.

SMASH BURGERS FOR EVERYONE

Classic Smash Burger

- 1 pound ground beef (80/20 mix for best flavor)
- Salt and freshly ground black pepper
- 4 slices American cheese
- 4 hamburger buns, toasted
- Lettuce leaves
- Tomato slices

For the Secret Burger Sauce:
- 1/4 cup mayonnaise
- 1 tablespoon ketchup
- 1 tablespoon yellow mustard
- 1 tablespoon relish
- 1 teaspoon white vinegar
- 1/4 teaspoon garlic powder
- 1/4 teaspoon onion powder
- Salt and pepper to taste

PREP. TIME: 10 min

COOKING TIME: 8 min

SERVES: 4

1. **Make the Burger Sauce**: In a small bowl, combine mayonnaise, ketchup, mustard, relish, vinegar, garlic powder, and onion powder. Stir until well mixed. Season with salt and pepper to taste. Set aside.
2. **Preheat the Griddle**: Heat your Blackstone griddle to high heat (about 400°F).
3. **Form and Season Patties**: Divide the ground beef into four equal portions. Roll each portion into a ball and season generously with salt and pepper.
4. **Cook the Burgers**: Place the beef balls on the hot griddle. Use a heavy spatula to smash each ball down into a flat patty. Let them cook without moving for about 3 minutes or until the edges are crispy and browned. Flip the patties, immediately place a slice of American cheese on each, and cook for an additional 2-3 minutes, or until the cheese is melted and the patties are cooked to your liking.
5. **Assemble the Burgers**: Spread a generous amount of the secret burger sauce on each toasted bun. Place a lettuce leaf and a slice of tomato on the bottom buns. Top with the hot, cheesy beef patties, then cover with the top buns.
6. **Serve**: Serve the smash burgers immediately while hot and juicy.

Bacon and Blue Cheese Smash Burger

- 1 pound ground beef (preferably 80/20 for juiciness)
- 4 slices bacon, cooked and crumbled
- Salt and freshly ground black pepper
- 4 ounces blue cheese, crumbled
- 1 large onion, thinly sliced
- 1 tablespoon butter
- 4 hamburger buns, toasted
- Optional: lettuce and tomato slices for garnish

PREP. TIME: 15 min

COOKING TIME: 10 min

SERVES: 4

1. **Prepare Caramelized Onions**: Melt butter over medium heat in a skillet or on one side of the Blackstone griddle. Add the thinly sliced onions and cook, stirring frequently, until they are golden brown and caramelized, about 10-15 minutes. Set aside.
2. **Mix Patties**: In a bowl, combine the ground beef, crumbled bacon, salt, and pepper. Mix gently to distribute the bacon evenly without overworking the meat.
3. **Preheat the Griddle**: Heat your Blackstone griddle to high heat (around 400°F).
4. **Form and Cook Patties**: Divide the beef mixture into four equal portions. Place each portion on the hot griddle and smash flat with a heavy spatula into a thin patty. Cook for about 3 minutes until the edges are crispy and browned. Flip the patties and immediately top each with crumbled blue cheese. Cook for an additional 2-3 minutes until the cheese melts and the patties are cooked to your preference.
5. **Assemble the Burgers**: Place each patty on a toasted bun. Top with caramelized onions and optional lettuce and tomato slices.
6. **Serve**: Close the burgers with the top buns and serve immediately while hot and juicy.

Spicy Jalapeño Smash Burger

PREP. TIME: 15 min

COOKING TIME: 8 min

SERVES: 4

- 1 pound ground beef (80/20 blend for best flavor)
- 2 jalapeños, finely diced (remove seeds for less heat)
- Salt and freshly ground black pepper

- 4 slices pepper jack cheese
- 1 avocado, thinly sliced
- 4 hamburger buns, toasted
- Optional garnishes: lettuce, tomato slices, and a dollop of sour cream or ranch dressing

1. **Prepare the Patties**: In a bowl, combine the ground beef, diced jalapeños, salt, and black pepper. Mix gently to incorporate the jalapeños evenly throughout the meat.
2. **Preheat the Griddle**: Heat your Blackstone griddle to high heat (around 400°F).
3. **Form and Cook Patties**: Divide the beef mixture into four equal portions. Place each portion on the hot griddle and use a heavy spatula to smash each ball down into a thin patty. Cook without moving for about 3-4 minutes or until the edges are crispy and browned. Flip the patties, place a slice of pepper jack cheese on each, and cook for an additional 3-4 minutes until the cheese is melted and the patties are cooked to your liking.
4. **Assemble the Burgers**: Place optional lettuce and tomato, if using, on the bottom half of each toasted bun. Add the cooked patty with melted cheese. Top with avocado slices and an optional sour cream or ranch dressing dollop to balance the heat.
5. **Serve**: Cap with the top halves of the buns and serve immediately while hot and juicy.

Mushroom Swiss Smash Burger

PREP. TIME: 15 min

COOKING TIME: 10 min

SERVES: 4

- 1 pound ground beef (80/20 mix for best flavor)
- Salt and freshly ground black pepper
- 8 ounces mushrooms, sliced
- 1 tablespoon butter
- 4 slices Swiss cheese
- 4 hamburger buns, toasted

For the Garlic Aioli:
- 1/2 cup mayonnaise
- 2 cloves garlic, minced
- 1 tablespoon lemon juice
- Salt and pepper to taste

1. **Make the Garlic Aioli**: In a small bowl, combine mayonnaise, minced garlic, and lemon juice. Season with salt and pepper to taste, mix well, and set aside.
2. **Sauté the Mushrooms**: Heat butter on the Blackstone griddle over medium heat. Add the sliced mushrooms and sauté until they are golden brown and tender, about 5-7 minutes. Remove from the griddle and set aside.
3. **Preheat the Griddle**: Increase the griddle temperature to high heat (around 400°F).
4. **Prepare and Cook the Patties**: Season the ground beef with salt and pepper and divide into four equal portions. Place each portion on the hot griddle and smash flat with a heavy spatula into a thin patty. Cook for about 3 minutes until the edges are crispy. Flip the patties, place a slice of Swiss cheese on each, and cook for another 3 minutes until the cheese is melted and the patties are cooked to your preference.
5. **Assemble the Burgers**: Spread garlic aioli on the bottom halves of the toasted buns. Place a cooked patty on each bun, top with sautéed mushrooms, and add more aioli if desired.
6. **Serve**: Close the burgers with the top halves of the buns and serve immediately while the flavors are rich and the patties are

BBQ Smash Burger

PREP. TIME: 15 min

COOKING TIME: 8 min

SERVES: 4

- 1 pound ground beef (80/20 mix for optimal flavor and juiciness)
- Salt and freshly ground black pepper
- 4 slices cheddar cheese
- 1 cup crispy fried onions

- 1/2 cup barbecue sauce
- 4 hamburger buns, toasted

1. **Prepare the Patties**: Season the ground beef with salt and pepper. Divide the beef into four equal portions. Roll each portion into a ball.
2. **Preheat the Griddle**: Heat your Blackstone griddle to high heat (around 400°F).
3. **Cook the Patties**: Place the balls of beef on the hot griddle. A heavy spatula smashes each ball into a flat patty about 1/2 inch thick. Cook for about 3-4 minutes until the edges are crispy and the bottom is nicely seared. Flip the patties and immediately place a slice of cheddar cheese on each. Cook for another 3-4 minutes until the cheese is melted and the patties are cooked to your preference.
4. **Assemble the Burgers**: Spread a generous barbecue sauce on each toasted bun's bottom half. Place the cooked patty on top of the sauce. Add a layer of crispy fried onions over the cheese.
5. **Serve**: Cap with the top halves of the buns and serve the burgers hot and juicy, ensuring each bite is packed with BBQ flavors.

Salmon Smash Burger

- 1 pound fresh salmon, skin removed and finely chopped
- 1 tablespoon fresh dill, finely chopped, plus extra for garnish
- Zest of 1 lemon
- Salt and freshly ground black pepper
- 1/4 cup breadcrumbs
- 1 egg, beaten
- 4 brioche buns, toasted
- Lettuce leaves for serving

For the Dill Yogurt Sauce:
- 1 cup Greek yogurt
- 2 tablespoons fresh dill, finely chopped
- 1 tablespoon lemon juice
- Salt and pepper to taste

PREP. TIME: 20 min

COOKING TIME: 8 min

SERVES: 4

1. **Prepare the Salmon Patties**: In a mixing bowl, combine the finely chopped salmon, 1 tablespoon of chopped dill, lemon zest, breadcrumbs, and beaten egg. Season with salt and pepper. Mix gently until the ingredients are well combined. Divide the mixture into four equal portions and shape into balls.
2. **Make the Dill Yogurt Sauce**: In a small bowl, mix together the Greek yogurt, 2 tablespoons of chopped dill, lemon juice, salt, and pepper. Stir until smooth and set aside.
3. **Preheat the Griddle**: Heat your Blackstone griddle to medium-high heat (around 375°F).
4. **Cook the Salmon Patties**: Place the salmon balls on the hot griddle. A spatula smashes each ball into a patty about 1/2 inch thick. Cook for about 4 minutes on each side or until golden brown patties are cooked through.
5. **Assemble the Burgers**: Spread a generous amount of the dill yogurt sauce on the bottom half of each toasted brioche bun. Place a salmon patty on top, add a few lettuce leaves, and garnish with additional dill if desired.
6. **Serve**: Top with the other half of the brioche bun and serve immediately. The dill and lemon enhance the salmon's fresh flavors, making this burger both refreshing and satisfying.

Tuna Melt Smash Burger

- 1 pound fresh tuna steaks, finely chopped
- 1 tablespoon Old Bay seasoning
- Salt and freshly ground black pepper to taste
- 4 slices Swiss cheese
- 4 hamburger buns, toasted
- Olive oil for grilling

For the Tartar Sauce:
- 1 cup mayonnaise
- 1/4 cup pickles, finely chopped
- 1 tablespoon capers, chopped
- 1 tablespoon lemon juice
- 1 teaspoon Dijon mustard
- Salt and pepper to taste

PREP. TIME: 15 min

COOKING TIME: 6 min

SERVES: 4

1. **Prepare the Tuna Patties**: In a mixing bowl, combine the finely chopped tuna, Old Bay seasoning, salt, and black pepper. Mix gently until well combined. Divide the mixture into four equal portions and form each into a loose ball.
2. **Make the Tartar Sauce**: In a small bowl, combine mayonnaise, chopped pickles, capers, lemon juice, and Dijon mustard. Season with salt and pepper to taste. Mix well and set aside.
3. **Preheat the Griddle**: Heat your Blackstone griddle to medium-high heat (around 375°F). Brush lightly with olive oil.
4. **Cook the Tuna Patties**: Place the tuna balls on the hot griddle. Use a spatula to smash each ball into a patty about 1/2 inch thick. Cook for about 3 minutes on each side or until the patties are cooked through and lightly browned.
5. **Add Cheese**: After flipping the patties, immediately place a slice of Swiss cheese on each and let it melt as the patties finish cooking.
6. **Assemble the Burgers**: Spread a generous amount of tartar sauce on the bottom halves of the toasted buns. Place the cooked tuna patties on top of the sauce, ensuring the melted cheese is uppermost.
7. **Serve**: Cap with the top halves of the buns and serve immediately while hot.

Plant-Powered Protein Smash Burger

PREP. TIME: 15 min
COOKING TIME: 8 min
SERVES: 4

- 4 plant-based burger patties (choose your favorite brand)
- Salt and freshly ground black pepper
- 4 slices vegan cheese
- 4 whole wheat or vegan hamburger buns, toasted

- Lettuce leaves
- Tomato slices
- Vegan mayonnaise
- Ketchup or preferred vegan burger sauce

1. **Preheat the Griddle**: Heat your Blackstone griddle to medium-high heat (around 375°F).
2. **Season and Cook Patties**: Lightly season the plant-based patties with salt and pepper. Place the patties on the griddle and press them down slightly to smash. Grill for about 4 minutes on each side or until they are browned and heated through.
3. **Add Cheese**: Place a slice of vegan cheese on each patty during the last minute of cooking to allow it to melt.
4. **Assemble the Burgers**: Spread vegan mayonnaise and ketchup (or your choice of sauce) on the bottom halves of the toasted buns. Place a lettuce leaf and a tomato slice on each bun, then add the cheese-topped patty.
5. **Serve**: Complete with the top halves of the buns. Serve immediately while hot and cheesy.

Vegan Black Bean Smash Burger

PREP. TIME: 20 min
COOKING TIME: 10 min
SERVES: 4

- 1 can (15 ounces) black beans, drained and rinsed
- 1/2 cup cooked quinoa
- 1 teaspoon ground cumin
- 1/2 teaspoon garlic powder
- 1/2 teaspoon smoked paprika
- Salt and freshly ground black pepper to taste
- 4 slices vegan cheese

- 4 whole wheat or gluten-free burger buns, toasted
- Olive oil for grilling

For the Spicy Vegan Mayo:
- 1/2 cup vegan mayonnaise
- 1 tablespoon hot sauce or to taste
- 1 teaspoon lime juice

1. **Prepare the Burger Patties**: Mash the black beans with a fork until smooth but with some whole beans left for texture. Stir in the cooked quinoa, cumin, garlic powder, smoked paprika, salt, and pepper. Mix well until combined.
2. **Make the Spicy Vegan Mayo**: In a small bowl, combine the vegan mayonnaise, hot sauce, and lime juice. Adjust the hot sauce to taste, mix well, and set aside.
3. **Preheat the Griddle**: Heat your Blackstone griddle to medium-high heat (around 375°F). Brush lightly with olive oil.
4. **Form and Cook the Patties**: Divide the bean and quinoa mixture into four equal portions. Place each portion on the hot griddle and use a spatula to smash it into a patty about 1/2 inch thick. Cook for about 5 minutes on each side or until the patties are crispy and heated through.
5. **Add Vegan Cheese**: After flipping the patties, immediately place a slice of vegan cheese on each and let it melt as the patties finish cooking.
6. **Assemble the Burgers**: Spread a generous amount of spicy vegan mayo on the bottom halves of the toasted buns. Place the cooked patties on top, and add any additional toppings such as lettuce, tomato, or avocado slices if desired.
7. **Serve**: Cap with the top halves of the buns and serve the burgers hot and crispy.

Chickpea and Spinach Smash Burger

PREP. TIME: 20 min
COOKING TIME: 10 min
SERVES: 4

- 1 can (15 ounces) chickpeas, drained and rinsed
- 1 cup fresh spinach, finely chopped
- 2 cloves garlic, minced
- 1 teaspoon ground cumin
- Salt and freshly ground black pepper to taste
- Olive oil for grilling
- 4 whole wheat or vegan burger buns, toasted

For the Vegan Tzatziki Sauce:
- 1 cup vegan yogurt
- 1 small cucumber, finely grated and excess water squeezed out
- 2 cloves garlic, minced
- 1 tablespoon fresh dill, chopped
- Juice of half a lemon
- Salt and pepper to taste

1. **Make Patties**: Mash chickpeas until mostly smooth, mix with spinach, garlic, cumin, salt, and pepper.
2. **Prepare Tzatziki**: Combine vegan yogurt, cucumber, garlic, dill, lemon juice, salt, and pepper; chill.
3. **Heat Griddle**: Set to medium-high (375°F) and oil lightly.
4. **Cook Patties**: Form mixture into four patties, smash onto the griddle, and cook 5 minutes per side until crispy.
5. **Assemble Burgers**: Spread tzatziki on buns, and add patties and optional toppings like tomato or lettuce.
6. **Serve**: Complete assembly with top bun and serve immediately.

WRAP, TACOS AND SANDWICHES

Carne Asada Tacos

- 1.5 pounds skirt steak or flank steak
- 3 tablespoons olive oil
- Juice of 2 limes
- 4 cloves garlic, minced
- 1 teaspoon ground cumin
- 1 teaspoon smoked paprika
- 1/2 teaspoon salt
- 1/2 teaspoon black pepper
- 1/4 cup fresh cilantro, chopped
- 8 corn tortillas
- 1 small white onion, finely chopped
- Additional fresh cilantro for garnish
- Lime wedges, for serving

PREP. TIME: 20 min

COOKING TIME: 10 min

SERVES: 4

1. **Marinate the Steak**: In a large bowl, combine olive oil, lime juice, minced garlic, cumin, smoked paprika, salt, pepper, and chopped cilantro. Add the steak, ensuring it is well coated with the marinade. Cover and refrigerate for at least 2 hours, preferably overnight.
2. **Preheat the Griddle**: Heat your Blackstone griddle to high heat (around 400°F).
3. **Grill the Steak**: Remove the steak from the marinade, letting excess drip off. Place the steak on the hot griddle and cook for about 5 minutes on each side for medium-rare or longer depending on thickness and desired doneness. Remove from the griddle and let rest for a few minutes.
4. **Prepare the Tortillas**: While the steak is resting, place the corn tortillas on the griddle for about 30 seconds per side, or until they are warm and slightly charred.
5. **Assemble the Tacos**: Slice the steak against the grain into thin strips. Place an even amount of steak on each warmed tortilla. Top with chopped onions and additional fresh cilantro.
6. **Serve**: Serve the tacos with lime wedges on the side for squeezing over the top.

Grilled Chicken Caesar Wrap

- 4 boneless, skinless chicken breasts
- Salt and freshly ground black pepper
- 2 tablespoons olive oil
- 4 large flour tortillas
- 1/2 cup Caesar dressing
- 2 cups chopped romaine lettuce
- 1/2 cup grated Parmesan cheese
- Optional: croutons for added crunch

PREP. TIME: 15 min

COOKING TIME: 10 min

SERVES: 4

1. **Season and Grill the Chicken**: Season the chicken breasts with salt and pepper, then brush with olive oil. Preheat your Blackstone griddle to medium-high heat (around 375°F). Place the chicken on the griddle and cook for about 5 minutes on each side, or until the internal temperature reaches 165°F and the outside is golden brown. Remove from the griddle and let rest for a few minutes before slicing thinly.
2. **Prepare the Wraps**: Lay out the flour tortillas on a clean surface. Spread a generous tablespoon of Caesar dressing over each tortilla.
3. **Assemble the Wraps**: Distribute the chopped romaine lettuce evenly among the tortillas. Add the sliced grilled chicken on top of the lettuce. Sprinkle grated Parmesan cheese over the chicken, and add croutons if desired.
4. **Roll the Wraps**: Fold the sides of the tortilla over the filling, then roll tightly from the bottom up to enclose all the ingredients.
5. **Serve**: Cut each wrap in half diagonally and serve immediately. Optionally, you can briefly grill the wraps on the Blackstone for 1-2 minutes on each side to toast the tortillas before serving.

Mediterranean Veggie Hummus Wrap

PREP. TIME: 15 min

COOKING TIME: 5 min

SERVES: 4

- 4 large whole wheat wraps
- 1 cup hummus
- 1 cup mixed greens (like spinach and arugula)
- 1 cucumber, thinly sliced
- 1 cup cherry tomatoes, halved
- 1/2 cup Kalamata olives, pitted and sliced
- 1/2 cup feta cheese, crumbled
- 1/4 cup red onion, thinly sliced
- 1/4 cup fresh parsley, chopped
- Salt and pepper, to taste
- Optional: drizzle of olive oil and a squeeze of lemon juice

1. **Prepare the Vegetables**: Wash and slice the cucumber, cherry tomatoes, and red onion. Chop the parsley. Set aside.
2. **Assemble the Wraps**: Lay out the whole wheat wraps on a clean, flat surface. Spread a generous layer of hummus on each wrap, leaving a small border around the edges.
3. **Add the Fillings**: On top of the hummus, evenly distribute the mixed greens, sliced cucumber, halved cherry tomatoes, sliced olives, crumbled feta cheese, and sliced red onion across each wrap.
4. **Season and Garnish**: Sprinkle salt and pepper to taste. Add the chopped parsley, and if desired, a light drizzle of olive oil and a squeeze of lemon juice for extra freshness.
5. **Roll the Wraps**: Carefully fold the sides of the wrap inward over the fillings and then roll tightly from the bottom up to enclose all the ingredients securely.
6. **Grill the Wraps** (Optional): For a warm, crispy exterior, place the wrapped tortillas on the preheated Blackstone griddle at medium heat. Grill for about 2-3 minutes on each side or until the wraps are golden brown and slightly crispy.
7. **Serve**: Cut each wrap in half diagonally and serve immediately. Enjoy a burst of Mediterranean flavors in each bite!

Buffalo Shrimp Tacos

PREP. TIME: 20 min

COOKING TIME: 10 min

SERVES: 4

- 1 pound large shrimp, peeled and deveined
- 1/2 cup buffalo sauce
- 1 tablespoon olive oil
- 8 small flour tortillas
- 1/2 cup blue cheese crumbles
- 1 cup shredded lettuce
- 1/2 cup thinly sliced celery
- 1/4 cup ranch dressing
- Lime wedges, for serving

1. **Marinate the Shrimp**: Toss the shrimp with the buffalo sauce in a medium bowl. Let them marinate for about 10 minutes to absorb the flavors.
2. **Preheat the Griddle**: Heat your Blackstone griddle to medium-high heat (around 375°F) and brush it lightly with olive oil.
3. **Cook the Shrimp**: Place the marinated shrimp on the hot griddle and cook for about 2-3 minutes per side, or until the shrimp are pink, firm, and cooked through.
4. **Warm the Tortillas**: While the shrimp are cooking, place the flour tortillas on the griddle for about 30 seconds on each side, just until they are warm and slightly charred.
5. **Assemble the Tacos**: Divide the shredded lettuce and sliced celery among the warmed tortillas. Place an even amount of cooked shrimp on top of the lettuce and celery. Sprinkle blue cheese crumbles over the shrimp.
6. **Serve**: Drizzle ranch dressing over each taco. Serve immediately with lime wedges on the side for squeezing over the tacos.

BBQ Pulled Pork Sandwiches

PREP. TIME: 30 min

COOKING TIME: 10 min

SERVES: 4

- 2 pounds pork shoulder
- 1 tablespoon salt
- 1 tablespoon smoked paprika
- 1 teaspoon garlic powder
- 1 teaspoon onion powder
- 1/2 teaspoon black pepper
- 1 cup barbecue sauce, plus extra for serving
- 4 hamburger buns, toasted
- 2 cups coleslaw
- Optional: pickles for garnish

1. **Prepare the Pork**: Rub the pork shoulder with salt, smoked paprika, garlic powder, onion powder, and black pepper. Cook the pork on your Blackstone griddle with a dome cover or in a slow cooker at low heat until it is very tender and shreds easily, typically about 6-8 hours.
2. **Shred the Pork**: Once cooked and slightly cooled, shred the pork using two forks, removing any excess fat.
3. **Mix with BBQ Sauce**: Return the shredded pork to the griddle or keep it in the slow cooker. Add the barbecue sauce and mix well, allowing it to warm through and absorb the flavors for about 10 minutes.
4. **Prepare the Coleslaw**: While the pork is warming with the sauce, mix shredded cabbage and carrots with coleslaw dressing until well combined.
5. **Assemble the Sandwiches**: Spoon a generous amount of the pulled pork onto each toasted hamburger bun. Top with a heap of coleslaw and extra BBQ sauce if desired.
6. **Serve**: Add pickles if using, and cover with the top of the bun. Serve immediately while warm.

BEEF AND STEAK RECIPES

Chopped Steak with Onion Gravy

For the Chopped Steak:
- 1 1/2 pounds ground beef (preferably 80/20 for juiciness)
- 1/2 cup breadcrumbs
- 1 egg
- 1 teaspoon garlic powder
- 1 teaspoon onion powder
- Salt and freshly ground black pepper
- 2 tablespoons olive oil

For the Onion Gravy:
- 2 large onions, thinly sliced
- 2 tablespoons butter
- 1 tablespoon flour
- 2 cups beef broth
- 1 teaspoon Worcestershire sauce
- Salt and pepper to taste

PREP. TIME: 15 min

COOKING TIME: 25 min

SERVES: 4

1. **Prepare the Steak Patties**: In a bowl, mix ground beef, breadcrumbs, egg, garlic powder, onion powder, salt, and pepper until well combined. Form into 4 oval patties about 3/4 inch thick.
2. **Cook the Patties**: Preheat the griddle to medium-high heat (about 375°F). Heat olive oil on the griddle. Cook patties 4-5 minutes per side until browned and cooked through. Remove and set aside.
3. **Caramelize Onions**: Reduce the griddle temperature to medium (about 350°F). Add butter and onions; cook, stirring frequently, until golden brown and caramelized, about 10-12 minutes.
4. **Make the Gravy**: Sprinkle flour over caramelized onions, stirring to combine. Cook for 1-2 minutes. Gradually stir in beef broth to avoid forming lumps. Add Worcestershire sauce. Season with salt and pepper. Allow to simmer until thickened, about 5 minutes.
5. **Combine and Simmer**: Return patties to the griddle, placing them into the onion gravy. Spoon gravy over the patties. Simmer on low heat (about 325°F) for 5 minutes to allow flavors to meld.
6. **Serve**: Serve the chopped steaks topped with generous amounts of onion gravy. Suggested accompaniments include mashed potatoes, steamed vegetables, or a fresh salad.

Ribeye Mongolian Beef

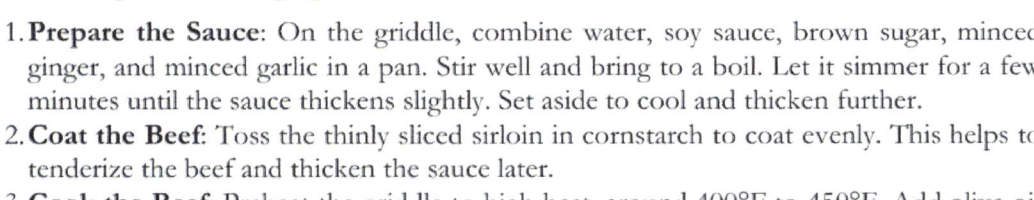

- 1 to 1.5 pounds sirloin steak, thinly sliced
- 1/4 cup cornstarch
- 2 tablespoons olive oil (for the griddle)

For the Sauce:
- 1/4 cup water
- 1/2 cup soy sauce
- 1/3 cup brown sugar
- 1 tablespoon minced ginger
- 3 cloves garlic, minced

For Serving:
- Cooked rice
- Sesame seeds (for garnish)
- Green onions, sliced (for garnish)

PREP. TIME: 15 min

COOKING TIME: 10 min

SERVES: 4

1. **Prepare the Sauce**: On the griddle, combine water, soy sauce, brown sugar, minced ginger, and minced garlic in a pan. Stir well and bring to a boil. Let it simmer for a few minutes until the sauce thickens slightly. Set aside to cool and thicken further.
2. **Coat the Beef**: Toss the thinly sliced sirloin in cornstarch to coat evenly. This helps to tenderize the beef and thicken the sauce later.
3. **Cook the Beef**: Preheat the griddle to high heat, around 400°F to 450°F. Add olive oil to the griddle. Once hot, add the beef slices. Cook quickly, moving the beef around on the griddle to ensure it cooks evenly and doesn't burn.
4. **Add the Sauce**: When the beef is nearly cooked through, pour the prepared sauce over it. Continue to cook, stirring for another minute to ensure the beef is well coated and the sauce is evenly distributed.
5. **Serve**: Spoon the cooked beef over a bed of cooked rice. Garnish with sesame seeds and sliced green onions.
6. **Enjoy**: Serve hot, perhaps lamenting the absence of chopsticks if you're eating it outdoors after a good hike, as suggested by the chefs!

Philly Cheesesteak

PREP. TIME: 10 min
COOKING TIME: 10 min
SERVES: 4

- 1 pound ribeye steak, thinly sliced
- 1 large onion, thinly sliced
- 1 green bell pepper, thinly sliced (optional)
- Salt and pepper to taste
- 4 tablespoons olive oil
- 4 slices provolone cheese
- 4 hoagie rolls, split and lightly toasted

1. **Preheat the Griddle**: Heat your Blackstone griddle to medium-high heat (around 375°F). Drizzle olive oil over the surface.
2. **Cook the Vegetables**: Add the sliced onions and bell peppers to the griddle. Season with salt and pepper. Cook, stirring frequently, until they are soft and slightly caramelized, about 5-7 minutes. Push the vegetables to one side of the griddle.
3. **Grill the Steak**: Place the thinly sliced ribeye steak on the griddle. Season with salt and pepper. Cook for 2-3 minutes, stirring frequently, until the steak is browned and cooked.
4. **Combine Ingredients**: Mix the cooked steak with the caramelized onions and bell peppers on the griddle. Divide the mixture into four equal portions.
5. **Add Cheese**: Place a slice of provolone cheese over each portion. Let the cheese melt into the steak and vegetables, about 1-2 minutes.
6. **Assemble the Sandwiches**: Open the toasted hoagie rolls and scoop each portion of the steak, cheese, and vegetable mixture into the rolls.
7. **Serve**: The Philly cheesesteaks should be served hot, optionally with ketchup, mayonnaise, or additional toppings of your choice.

Grilled Tomahawk Ribeye Steak

PREP. TIME: 10 min
COOKING TIME: 20 min
SERVES: 2-3

- 1 Tomahawk ribeye steak (about 2-2.5 inches thick)
- Salt (preferably coarse or kosher)
- Freshly ground black pepper
- 2 tablespoons olive oil
- 3 cloves garlic, minced
- Fresh rosemary sprigs
- Butter (optional, for finishing)

1. **Season and Rest**: Let the steak reach room temperature, then season generously with salt and pepper.
2. **Heat the Griddle**: Preheat the Blackstone to high (450°F to 500°F). Drizzle olive oil, where you'll cook the steak.
3. **Sear the Steak**: Place the steak on the griddle with garlic and rosemary. Sear for 4-5 minutes per side to form a crust. If needed, also sear the fat side.
4. **Lower Heat and Cook**: Reduce heat to medium-low (around 300°F). Cover with a lid or foil and cook for 10-15 minutes, until an internal temperature of 125°F for medium-rare is reached.
5. **Rest and Serve**: Remove the steak, rest for 10 minutes with optional butter on top. Slice against the grain and serve.

New York Strip Steak with Garlic Butter

PREP. TIME: 5 min
COOKING TIME: 10 min
SERVES: 2

- 2 New York strip steaks (about 1-inch thick)
- Salt, to taste
- Freshly ground black pepper, to taste
- 2 tablespoons olive oil
- 4 tablespoons butter
- 3 cloves garlic, minced
- 1 tablespoon fresh parsley, finely chopped

1. **Season the Steak**: Allow the steaks to sit at room temperature for about 20-30 minutes before cooking. Season both sides generously with salt and freshly ground black pepper.
2. **Preheat the Griddle**: Heat your Blackstone griddle over high heat until it's very hot, around 400°F to 450°F.
3. **Cook the Steak**: Drizzle olive oil over the hot griddle. Place the steaks on the griddle and cook for about 4-5 minutes on each side for medium-rare, or adjust the time depending on your preferred level of doneness. This high heat will give the steaks a nice sear.
4. **Make the Garlic Butter**: While the steaks are cooking, melt the butter in a small skillet or on another part of the griddle. Add the minced garlic and sauté until fragrant, about 1-2 minutes. Remove from heat and stir in the chopped parsley.
5. **Rest the Steak**: Once the steaks are cooked to your liking, transfer them to a plate and let them rest for about 5 minutes. This helps the juices redistribute throughout the meat, keeping it juicy and flavorful.
6. **Serve**: Spoon the garlic butter over the steaks while they are still warm, letting the butter melt and coat the steak with its garlicky, herby richness.
7. **Enjoy**: Serve your garlic butter-topped New York strip steaks with sides of your choice, such as baked potatoes, steamed vegetables, or a simple salad.

T-Bone Steak with Crispy Potatoes

- T-Bone steaks (3-pack)
- Mini red potatoes, washed and halved
- Avocado oil
- Steakhouse seasoning
- Blackened steak seasoning
- Garlic paste
- Fresh parsley, chopped (curly or flat leaf)
- Butter
- Salt and pepper, to taste

PREP. TIME: 10 min

COOKING TIME: 30 min

SERVES: 4

1. **Season and Rest the Steaks**: Let the steaks reach room temperature for 20-30 minutes. Coat with avocado oil, then generously season with steakhouse and blackened steak seasonings. Add garlic paste.
2. **Preheat the Griddle**: Set the Blackstone griddle high, reaching 400°F to 450°F.
3. **Cook the Steaks**: Sear for 4-5 minutes per side for medium-rare (130°F to 135°F). Adjust time for desired doneness.
4. **Prepare the Potatoes**: Arrange potatoes in a circle on the griddle, add water, and cover to steam. After 7-8 minutes, uncover, spread out, and season.
5. **Make the Garlic Butter**: Melt butter on the griddle, mix in garlic paste, and sauté until fragrant. Stir in parsley and remove from heat.
6. **Rest the Steaks**: Transfer steaks to a plate to rest for 5 minutes.
7. **Serve**: Drizzle garlic butter over steaks and garnish potatoes with parsley.
8. **Enjoy**: Serve steaks and potatoes hot, with garlic butter enhancing the flavors.

Filet Mignon with Blue Cheese and Asparagus

- 2 filet mignon steaks
- Salt, to taste
- Black pepper, to taste
- Beef tallow, for searing
- Asparagus ends trimmed
- Avocado oil
- Garlic butter seasoning (or your choice of seasoning)
- Blue cheese crumbles
- Water, for steaming

PREP. TIME: 10 min

COOKING TIME: 20 min

SERVES: 2

1. **Season the Steak**: Let steaks sit at room temperature for about 20-30 minutes before cooking—season generously with salt and black pepper.
2. **Preheat the Griddle**: Heat your Blackstone griddle over high heat to 500°F to 700°F, ensuring it's hot enough for a good sear.
3. **Cook the Steak**: Add beef tallow to the griddle and place the steaks down, searing each side for about 4-5 minutes or until desired doneness is achieved, aiming for a medium-rare finish (internal temperature of 130°F to 135°F).
4. **Optionally**: sear the edges of the steaks by standing them on their sides.
5. **Prepare the Asparagus**: Toss asparagus in avocado oil and seasoning, then cook on the griddle until tender, stirring occasionally.
6. **Melt Blue Cheese on Steak**: Move steaks to a warming rack. Top each steak with blue cheese crumbles, add water to the griddle, and cover with a basting cover. Steam for about 45 seconds or until the cheese melts beautifully.
7. **Serve**: Arrange the asparagus on plates. Place the blue cheese-topped filets alongside. Check steak doneness and adjust by cooking a bit longer if needed.
8. **Enjoy**: Serve this elegant dish for a special Valentine's Day meal, impressing your loved one with a perfectly cooked filet mignon and flavorful sides.

POULTRY RECIPES

Grilled Chicken Breasts with Herb Marinade

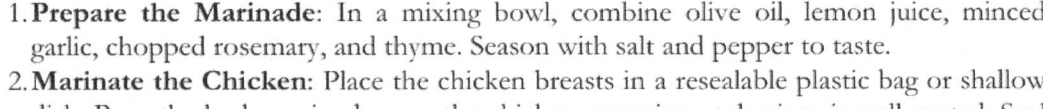

- 4 boneless, skinless chicken breasts
- 1/4 cup olive oil
- Juice of 1 lemon
- 3 cloves garlic, minced
- 1 tablespoon fresh rosemary, finely chopped
- 1 tablespoon fresh thyme, finely chopped
- Salt and freshly ground black pepper, to taste

PREP. TIME: 10 min

COOKING TIME: 12-14 min

SERVES: 4

1. **Prepare the Marinade**: In a mixing bowl, combine olive oil, lemon juice, minced garlic, chopped rosemary, and thyme. Season with salt and pepper to taste.
2. **Marinate the Chicken**: Place the chicken breasts in a resealable plastic bag or shallow dish. Pour the herb marinade over the chicken, ensuring each piece is well coated. Seal or cover, and refrigerate for at least 1 hour, preferably longer for deeper flavor.
3. **Preheat the Griddle**: Heat your Blackstone griddle to medium-high heat, around 375°F to 400°F.
4. **Grill the Chicken**: Remove the chicken from the marinade, letting the excess drip off. Place the chicken breasts on the hot griddle. Grill for 6-7 minutes on each side or until the chicken is golden brown on the outside and reaches an internal temperature of 165°F.
5. **Rest the Chicken**: Once cooked, transfer the chicken breasts to a plate and let them rest for a few minutes. This helps retain their juices, making the chicken moist and tender.
6. **Serve**: Slice the chicken if desired, and serve hot. This dish pairs well with a variety of sides such as grilled vegetables, a fresh salad, or over cooked pasta.

BBQ Chicken Thighs

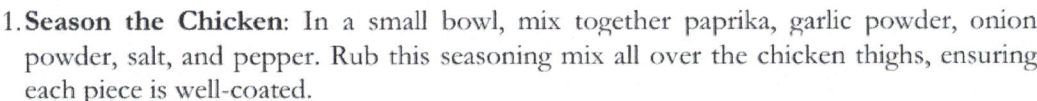

- 8 chicken thighs, bone-in, skin-on
- 1 tablespoon paprika
- 1 teaspoon garlic powder
- 1 teaspoon onion powder
- Salt and freshly ground black pepper, to taste
- 1 cup BBQ sauce (choose your favorite brand)
- Olive oil for brushing

PREP. TIME: 10 min

COOKING TIME: 20 min

SERVES: 4

1. **Season the Chicken**: In a small bowl, mix together paprika, garlic powder, onion powder, salt, and pepper. Rub this seasoning mix all over the chicken thighs, ensuring each piece is well-coated.
2. **Preheat the Griddle**: Heat your Blackstone griddle to medium-high heat, around 375°F to 400°F. Brush the griddle lightly with olive oil to prevent sticking.
3. **Grill the Chicken**: Place the chicken thighs skin-side down on the griddle. Cook for about 10 minutes, then flip the thighs over. Continue to grill for another 10 minutes, or until the chicken is nearly cooked through and the skin is crispy.
4. **Apply BBQ Sauce**: During the last 5 minutes of cooking, brush a generous amount of BBQ sauce on each chicken thigh. Flip the thighs several times and apply more sauce with each turn to build a rich glaze.
5. **Check Doneness**: Ensure the chicken thighs are fully cooked and reach an internal temperature of 165°F when checked with a meat thermometer.
6. **Rest and Serve**: Let the chicken rest for a few minutes off the griddle before serving. This helps the juices settle, making the chicken more moist and flavorful.
7. **Enjoy**: Serve the BBQ chicken thighs hot, with extra BBQ sauce on the side for dipping, and perhaps some grilled vegetables or a fresh coleslaw as accompaniments.

Buffalo Chicken Grilled Cheese

PREP. TIME: 15 min

COOKING TIME: 10 min

SERVES: 4

- 2 cups cooked chicken, shredded
- 1/2 cup buffalo sauce
- 8 slices of bread (sourdough or your choice)
- 4 tablespoons butter, softened
- 8 slices cheddar cheese or a mix of cheddar and blue cheese for extra flavor
- Optional garnishes: ranch or blue cheese dressing for dipping

1. **Prepare the Buffalo** Chicken: Combine the shredded chicken with buffalo sauce, ensuring the chicken is evenly coated.
2. **Butter and Assemble Sandwiches**: Spread butter on one side of each slice of bread. Lay the buttered side down on a clean surface. Place a slice of cheese on each of four bread slices. Evenly distribute the buffalo chicken on top of the cheese. Top the chicken with another slice of cheese and cover with the remaining bread slices, buttered side up.
3. **Grill the Sandwiches**: Preheat your Blackstone griddle to medium heat (about 350°F). Place the sandwiches on the griddle and cook for about 4-5 minutes on each side or until the bread is golden brown and the cheese has melted.
4. **Serve**: Cut the grilled cheese sandwiches in half and serve hot, with ranch or blue cheese dressing on the side for dipping if desired.

Teriyaki Chicken Skewers

PREP. TIME: 20 min

COOKING TIME: 10 min

SERVES: 4

- 1.5 pounds chicken breast, cut into 1-inch cubes
- 1 cup teriyaki sauce (store-bought or homemade)
- 1 red bell pepper, cut into 1-inch pieces
- 1 green bell pepper, cut into 1-inch pieces
- 1 large onion, cut into 1-inch pieces
- Wooden or metal skewers

1. **Marinate the Chicken**: Place the chicken cubes in a large bowl or resealable plastic bag. Pour the teriyaki sauce over the chicken, ensuring all pieces are well-coated. Refrigerate and let marinate for at least 2 hours, or overnight for best results.
2. **Preheat the Griddle**: Heat your Blackstone griddle to medium-high heat (around 375°F).
3. **Prepare the Skewers**: If using wooden skewers, soak them in water for at least 30 minutes before grilling to prevent burning. Thread the marinated chicken, bell peppers, and onions alternately onto the skewers.
4. **Grill the Skewers**: Place the skewers on the hot griddle. Grill for about 10 minutes, turning occasionally, until the chicken is thoroughly cooked and the vegetables are slightly charred and tender.
5. **Serve**: Remove the skewers from the griddle and let them rest for a few minutes. Serve hot, optionally, with extra teriyaki sauce for dipping or drizzling.

Lemon Garlic Chicken Wings

PREP. TIME: 10 min

COOKING TIME: 15 min

SERVES: 4

- 2 pounds chicken wings, tips removed and drumettes separated
- 1/4 cup olive oil
- Zest of 1 lemon
- Juice of 2 lemons
- 4 cloves garlic, minced
- Salt and freshly ground black pepper, to taste
- Optional garnish: Chopped fresh parsley

1. **Marinate the Chicken**: In a large bowl, whisk together olive oil, lemon zest, lemon juice, minced garlic, salt, and pepper. Add the chicken wings and toss until they are well coated. Cover and refrigerate to marinate for at least 1 hour, preferably longer for more flavor.
2. **Preheat the Griddle**: Heat your Blackstone griddle to medium heat (around 350°F).
3. **Cook the Wings**: Remove the chicken wings from the marinade, letting the excess drip off. Arrange the wings on the griddle and cook for 15-20 minutes, turning occasionally, until they are golden brown and cooked through. The wings should reach an internal temperature of 165°F.
4. **Serve**: Transfer the cooked chicken wings to a serving platter. If desired, sprinkle with chopped fresh parsley for added color and freshness.
5. **Enjoy**: Serve the lemon garlic chicken wings hot, possibly with extra lemon wedges for squeezing over the wings.

TURKEY RECIPES

Turkey and Veggie Fajitas

- 1 pound turkey breast, thinly sliced
- 2 bell peppers (one red, one green), sliced
- 1 large onion, sliced
- 2 tablespoons olive oil
- 2 tablespoons fajita seasoning
- Juice of 1 lime
- 8 flour tortillas
- Optional garnishes: salsa, sour cream, guacamole, shredded cheese

PREP. TIME: 20 min

COOKING TIME: 10 min

SERVES: 4

1. **Marinate Turkey**: In a large bowl, combine the thinly sliced turkey breast with 1 tablespoon of olive oil, fajita seasoning, and lime juice. Toss to coat evenly. Let marinate for at least 15 minutes to enhance the flavor.
2. **Preheat the Griddle**: Heat your Blackstone griddle to medium-high heat (about 375°F).
3. **Cook the Vegetables**: Drizzle the remaining tablespoon of olive oil onto the hot griddle. Add the sliced bell peppers and onion. Cook, stirring frequently, until the vegetables are tender and slightly charred, about 5-6 minutes. Remove from the griddle and set aside.
4. **Cook the Turkey**: Place the marinated turkey slices on the griddle. Cook, stirring occasionally, until the turkey is cooked through and slightly browned, about 4-5 minutes.
5. **Combine Ingredients**: Return the cooked vegetables to the griddle with the turkey. Stir everything together for an additional minute to mix the flavors.
6. **Warm the Tortillas**: Place the flour tortillas on the griddle for about 30 seconds per side until they are warm and pliable.
7. **Assemble the Fajitas**: Divide the turkey and vegetable mixture among the warm tortillas. Add any optional garnishes such as salsa, sour cream, guacamole, or shredded cheese.
8. **Serve**: Fold the tortillas over the filling and serve the fajitas hot, with lime wedges on the side for squeezing over the top if desired.

Turkey Meatloaf with BBQ Glaze

For the Meatloaf:
- 2 pounds of ground turkey
- 1 cup breadcrumbs
- 1/2 cup milk
- 1 large egg, beaten
- 1 medium onion, finely chopped
- 2 cloves garlic, minced
- 1 tablespoon Worcestershire sauce
- Salt and freshly ground black pepper to taste

For the BBQ Glaze:
- 1/2 cup ketchup
- 2 tablespoons brown sugar
- 1/4 cup BBQ sauce
- 1 teaspoon smoked paprika

PREP. TIME: 15 min

COOKING TIME: 1 h

SERVES: 6

1. **Prep Ingredients & Meatloaf**: Mix turkey, breadcrumbs (soaked in milk), egg, onion, garlic, Worcestershire sauce, salt, and pepper. Form into a loaf.
2. **Mix BBQ Glaze**: Combine ketchup, brown sugar, BBQ sauce, and paprika.
3. **Griddle Setup**: Heat griddle to 350°F on one side for indirect cooking.
4. **Cook Meatloaf**: Place meatloaf on the cooler side of the griddle. Apply half the glaze and cover with a lid or foil. Cook for 30 minutes.
5. **Glaze and Finish Cooking**: Apply the remaining glaze and cook for another 30 minutes or until the internal temperature reaches 165°F.
6. **Rest and Serve**: Let the meatloaf rest for 10 minutes, then slice and serve.

Turkey and Spinach Stuffed Shells

PREP. TIME: 20 min

COOKING TIME: 30 min

SERVES: 6

- 24 large pasta shells
- 1 pound ground turkey
- 2 cups fresh spinach, chopped
- 1 cup ricotta cheese
- 1/2 cup grated Parmesan cheese
- 1 large egg

- 2 cups marinara sauce
- 1 teaspoon garlic powder
- 1 teaspoon dried oregano
- Salt and freshly ground black pepper to taste
- 1 cup shredded mozzarella cheese

1. **Cook Pasta Shells**: Boil salted water, add pasta shells, cook until al dente (8-10 minutes), drain, and set aside to cool.
2. **Prepare the Filling**: Sauté ground turkey in a skillet over medium heat until no longer pink (5-7 minutes), and drain excess fat.
3. **Combine Ingredients**: In a large bowl, mix cooked turkey, chopped spinach, ricotta, Parmesan, egg, garlic powder, oregano, salt, and pepper.
4. **Preheat Oven**: Set oven to 375°F (190°C).
5. **Assemble Shells**: Spread 1 cup of marinara sauce in a baking dish. Stuff shells with turkey mixture and place in the dish.
6. **Top and Bake**: Cover shells with remaining marinara sauce, top with mozzarella, cover with foil, and bake for 20 minutes. Remove foil, bake another 10 minutes until cheese is bubbly and browned.
7. Serve: Cool briefly, garnish with Parmesan or herbs, and serve.

Turkey Sausage and Peppers

PREP. TIME: 15 min

COOKING TIME: 15 min

SERVES: 4

- 1.5 pounds of turkey sausage links
- 2 bell peppers, one red and one green, sliced
- 1 large onion, sliced
- 2 tablespoons olive oil
- Salt and freshly ground black pepper to taste
- Optional: hoagie rolls for serving

1. **Cook Pasta Shells**: Boil shells in salted water until al dente (8-10 minutes), drain, and cool.
2. **Prepare the Filling**: Sauté ground turkey until no longer pink (5-7 minutes), and drain.
3. **Combine Ingredients**: Mix turkey, spinach, ricotta, Parmesan, egg, garlic powder, oregano, salt, and pepper in a bowl.
4. **Preheat Oven**: Heat oven to 375°F (190°C).
5. **Assemble Shells**: Spread 1 cup of marinara sauce in a baking dish. Stuff the shells with the turkey mixture and arrange them in the dish.
6. **Top and Bake**: Cover with remaining marinara and mozzarella. Bake covered with foil for 20 minutes, then uncovered for 10 minutes until the cheese is bubbly.
7. **Serve**: Let cool briefly, garnish with Parmesan or herbs, and serve.

Lemon Herb Turkey Cutlets

PREP. TIME: 15 min

COOKING TIME: 6-8 min

SERVES: 4

- 1.5 pounds turkey breast cutlets
- Zest of 1 lemon
- Juice of 2 lemons
- 3 cloves garlic, minced
- 2 tablespoons fresh parsley, finely chopped

- 1 tablespoon fresh thyme, finely chopped
- 1 tablespoon fresh rosemary, finely chopped
- 1/4 cup olive oil
- Salt and freshly ground black pepper to taste

1. **Prepare the Marinade**: In a bowl, mix lemon zest, lemon juice, garlic, parsley, thyme, rosemary, olive oil, salt, and pepper.
2. **Marinate the Cutlets**: Coat turkey cutlets in the marinade, refrigerate in a sealed dish or bag for at least 30 minutes (longer for more flavor).
3. **Preheat the Griddle**: Set the Blackstone griddle to medium-high heat (375°F to 400°F).
4. **Cook the Cutlets**: Remove cutlets from the marinade and cook on the griddle for 3-4 minutes per side until golden brown and fully cooked (internal temperature of 165°F).
5. **Serve and Enjoy**: Place cutlets on a platter, garnish with herbs or lemon slices. Serve with steamed vegetables, salad, or grains like quinoa or rice.

PORK RECIPES

Crispy Grilled Pork Belly

- 2 pounds pork belly, skin scored
- 1/4 cup soy sauce
- 2 tablespoons honey
- 1 tablespoon rice vinegar
- 1 tablespoon sesame oil
- 4 cloves garlic, minced
- 1 inch piece ginger, grated
- 1 teaspoon chili flakes (optional for heat)
- Salt and freshly ground black pepper, to taste

PREP. TIME: 15 min (plus marinating time)
COOKING TIME: 20 min

SERVES: 4

1. **Marinate Pork Belly**: Mix soy sauce, honey, rice vinegar, sesame oil, garlic, ginger, and chili flakes. Score the pork belly skin, then marinate it in this mixture for at least 4 hours, preferably overnight.
2. **Preheat the Griddle**: Set the Blackstone griddle to medium heat (300°F to 350°F).
3. **Cook Pork Belly**: Remove pork belly from the marinade (reserve the marinade). Season with salt and pepper. Place skin-side down on the griddle, cook for 10 minutes, flip, and cook another 10 minutes, basting with reserved marinade.
4. **Crisp the Skin**: Increase heat to high for the final few minutes to crisp the skin, monitoring closely to prevent burning.
5. **Rest and Serve**: Let the pork belly rest for 5 minutes, then slice and serve. Enjoy as is, or with sides like rice or vegetables.

Grilled Beer-Marinated Pork Chops

- 4 bone-in pork chops, about 1-inch thick
- 1 can (12 oz) beer (a lager or ale works best)
- 1/4 cup olive oil
- 2 tablespoons soy sauce
- 2 cloves garlic, minced
- 1 tablespoon brown sugar
- 1 teaspoon smoked paprika
- 1 teaspoon black pepper
- Salt to taste

PREP. TIME: 10 min (plus 4-8 hours for marinating)

COOKING TIME: 12 min

SERVES: 4

1. **Prepare the Marinade**: In a large mixing bowl, combine the beer, olive oil, soy sauce, minced garlic, brown sugar, smoked paprika, and black pepper. Stir well to ensure all ingredients are fully integrated.
2. **Marinate the Pork Chops**: Place the pork chops in a resealable plastic bag or a shallow dish. Pour the marinade over the chops, ensuring they are well-coated. Seal the bag or cover the dish and refrigerate for at least 4 hours or overnight for best results.
3. **Preheat the Griddle**: Heat your Blackstone griddle to medium-high heat, approximately 375°F to 400°F.
4. **Grill the Pork Chops**: Remove the pork chops from the marinade, letting the excess drip off (discard the remaining marinade). Season the chops with salt to taste. Place them on the hot griddle and grill for about 6 minutes per side or until the internal temperature reaches 145°F. The chops should have a nice sear and be slightly charred on the edges.
5. **Rest and Serve**: Transfer the grilled pork chops to a plate and let them rest for about 5 minutes. This allows the juices to redistribute throughout the meat, ensuring that each chop is juicy and flavorful when sliced.
6. **Enjoy**: Serve the pork chops hot, perhaps with a side of grilled vegetables or a fresh salad to complement the rich flavors of the marinade.

Classic Grilled Pork Chops

PREP. TIME: 10 min

COOKING TIME: 14 min

SERVES: 6

- 4 bone-in pork chops, about 1-inch thick
- 2 tablespoons olive oil
- 1 teaspoon salt
- 1/2 teaspoon freshly ground black pepper
- 1/2 teaspoon garlic powder

1. **Prepare the Pork Chops**: Rub each pork chop with olive oil. In a small bowl, mix salt, pepper, and garlic powder. Sprinkle the seasoning mixture evenly over both sides of the pork chops.
2. **Preheat the Griddle**: Heat your Blackstone griddle to medium-high heat (around 375°F to 400°F).
3. **Grill the Pork Chops**: Place the seasoned pork chops on the hot griddle. Grill for about 7 minutes on one side. Flip the chops over and continue grilling for another 7 minutes on the other side, or until the internal temperature of the pork chops reaches 145°F as measured by a meat thermometer.
4. **Rest the Meat**: Remove the pork chops from the griddle and let them rest for 5 minutes. Resting helps the juices redistribute throughout the meat, ensuring that the pork chops are juicy and flavorful when sliced.
5. **Serve**: Serve the pork chops hot, optionally with sides like grilled vegetables, mashed potatoes, or a fresh salad.

Pork Tenderloin with Apple Balsamic Glaze

PREP. TIME: 15 min

COOKING TIME: 20 min

SERVES: 4

- 1 pork tenderloin (about 1 to 1.5 pounds)
- Salt and freshly ground black pepper to taste
- 2 tablespoons olive oil

For the Apple Balsamic Glaze:
- 1 cup apple cider
- 1/2 cup balsamic vinegar
- 2 tablespoons brown sugar
- 1 tablespoon Dijon mustard

1. **Season Pork**: Generously season the pork tenderloin with salt and pepper.
2. **Heat Griddle**: Preheat the Blackstone griddle to medium-high (375°F to 400°F).
3. **Cook Pork**: Brush the griddle with olive oil, place the pork on the griddle, and cook for about 20 minutes, turning occasionally, until the internal temperature reaches 145°F.
4. **Prepare Glaze**: Simmer apple cider, balsamic vinegar, and brown sugar in a saucepan until reduced by half (about 15 minutes). Stir in Dijon mustard.
5. **Apply Glaze**: Brush the pork with glaze during the last few minutes of cooking, turning frequently.
6. **Rest and Serve**: Remove pork from griddle, let rest for 5 minutes, slice, and serve drizzled with extra glaze.

Smoked Sausage and Peppers

PREP. TIME: 15 min

COOKING TIME: 20 min

SERVES: 4

- 2 lbs Louisiana smoked sausage, sliced
- 2 large bell peppers (one red, one green), cored and sliced
- 1 large onion, sliced
- 1/4 cup olive oil
- Cajun seasoning, to taste
- 4 hoagie rolls
- 1 cup shredded cheese (optional)
- Worcestershire sauce, a few splashes
- Butter, for buns
- Mustard, for serving
- Bayou blend spices, for garnish

1. **Preheat the Griddle**: Heat your Blackstone griddle to medium-high heat.
2. **Cook the Sausage**: Place the sliced sausages on the griddle. Add a little oil if necessary. Cook until they start to brown and are heated through, about 10 minutes, flipping occasionally.
3. **Sauté Vegetables**: In another area of the griddle, add a line of oil and then the sliced peppers and onions. Season with Cajun seasoning. Cook until they are soft and slightly charred, about 8-10 minutes. Occasionally, you can cover with a griddle dome to steam and speed up the cooking process.
4. **Combine Ingredients**: Once the vegetables are tender, mix them with the sausages on the griddle. Add a few splashes of Worcestershire sauce for extra flavor. Combine well.
5. **Warm the Buns**: Place the hoagie rolls on the Blackstone's warming tray to toast them slightly.
6. **Add Cheese and Final Seasoning**: Sprinkle cheese over the sausage and vegetable mixture, allowing it to melt. Once melted, sprinkle Bayou blend spices over the top for additional flavor.
7. **Assemble the Po-Boys**: Spread mustard inside the warmed hoagie rolls, then fill them with the cheesy sausage and pepper mixture.
8. **Serve**: Serve the Cajun Po-Boys hot, ensuring each bite is filled with the flavors of Louisiana.

STIR-FRY RECIPES

Chicken and Broccoli Stir-Fry

- 1.5 pounds chicken breast, thinly sliced
- 4 cups broccoli florets
- 2 tablespoons vegetable oil
- 1 tablespoon garlic, minced
- 1/4 cup soy sauce
- 2 tablespoons oyster sauce
- 1 tablespoon honey
- 1 teaspoon sesame oil
- 2 teaspoons cornstarch dissolved in 3 tablespoons water
- Salt and pepper, to taste

PREP. TIME: 15 min

COOKING TIME: 10 min

SERVES: 4

1. **Prepare Ingredients**: Slice chicken breast thinly. Chop broccoli into florets. Mix soy sauce, oyster sauce, honey, and sesame oil for the sauce. Dissolve cornstarch in water for the slurry.
2. **Preheat Griddle**: Heat Blackstone gas griddle to medium-high (375°F).
3. **Cook Chicken**: Drizzle oil on the griddle. Cook chicken slices for 2-3 minutes per side until golden. Set aside.
4. **Cook Broccoli**: Add oil if needed and cook broccoli for 3-4 minutes until crisp-tender.
5. **Add Garlic**: Cook minced garlic until fragrant, about 1 minute.
6. **Combine and Sauce**: Return chicken to the griddle. Pour sauce over chicken and broccoli and stir to coat.
7. **Thicken Sauce**: Add cornstarch slurry and mix until sauce thickens, about 1-2 minutes.
8. **Serve**: Adjust seasoning with salt and pepper. Serve hot, optionally garnished with sesame seeds or green onions.

Cowboy Stir-Fry with Smoked Sausage and Potatoes

- pound smoked sausage, sliced
- 1 pound mixed baby potatoes (yellow and red), halved
- 1 large yellow onion, diced
- 1 red bell pepper, diced
- 2 medium zucchinis, chopped
- 1/4 cup olive oil
- 1 teaspoon paprika
- 1 teaspoon garlic powder
- 2 tablespoons Cajun seasoning
- Salt and pepper to taste
- Fresh parsley, chopped (for garnish)

PREP. TIME: 20 min

COOKING TIME: 25 min

SERVES: 4

1. **Preheat the Griddle**: Heat your Blackstone gas griddle to medium-high heat, around 375°F.
2. **Cook the Potatoes**: Place the halved baby potatoes on the griddle. Drizzle with half of the olive oil and season with paprika, garlic powder, and half of the Cajun seasoning. Toss to coat evenly. Cover with a dome or aluminum foil to steam, stirring occasionally, until they start to soften, about 10-15 minutes.
3. **Add Sausage and Veggies**: Add the smoked sausage slices to the griddle alongside the potatoes. Cook for about 5 minutes, then add the diced onion, red bell pepper, and zucchini. Drizzle the remaining olive oil over the vegetables and season with the remaining Cajun seasoning, salt, and pepper. Cook, stirring frequently, until the vegetables are tender and the sausage is browned, about 10 more minutes.
4. **Combine**: Mix everything on the griddle to blend the flavors once the vegetables are cooked and the potatoes are tender. Cook together for an additional 2-3 minutes.
5. **Garnish and Serve**: Remove from heat, garnish with fresh chopped parsley, and serve hot.
6. **Enjoy**: This Cowboy Stir-Fry captures the essence of a hearty, rustic meal that's perfect for a filling dinner or a social gathering around the griddle.

Beef and Bell Pepper Stir-Fry

PREP. TIME: 15 min
COOKING TIME: 10 min
SERVES: 4

- 1.5 pounds flank steak, thinly sliced against the grain
- 3 bell peppers (one each of red, green, and yellow), thinly sliced
- 1 large onion, thinly sliced
- 3 tablespoons vegetable oil
- 2 cloves garlic, minced
- 1/4 cup soy sauce

- 2 tablespoons oyster sauce
- 1 tablespoon brown sugar
- 1 teaspoon sesame oil
- Salt and freshly ground black pepper, to taste
- Optional: sesame seeds and sliced green onions for garnish

1. **Prepare Ingredients**: Thinly slice the flank steak and bell peppers. Combine soy sauce, oyster sauce, brown sugar, and sesame oil to make the sauce.
2. **Heat Griddle**: Set the Blackstone griddle to medium-high heat (375°F).
3. **Sauté Vegetables**: Add 2 tablespoons vegetable oil and sauté bell peppers and onion for 5 minutes until slightly softened.
4. **Cook Beef**: Add 1 tablespoon oil, then beef and garlic. Season with salt and pepper. Stir-fry for 3 minutes until browned.
5. **Combine and Finish**: Add sauce to the beef and vegetables. Stir-fry for 2 more minutes until the sauce thickens.
6. **Serve**: Garnish with sesame seeds and green onions if desired. Serve hot with rice or noodles.

Shrimp and Asparagus Stir-Fry

PREP. TIME: 15 min
COOKING TIME: 10 min
SERVES: 4

- 1 pound large shrimp, peeled and deveined
- 1 pound asparagus, trimmed and cut into 2-inch pieces
- 3 tablespoons olive oil
- 2 cloves garlic, minced
- 1 tablespoon ginger, minced
- 1/4 cup soy sauce

- 2 tablespoons oyster sauce
- 1 tablespoon honey
- 1 teaspoon sesame oil
- Salt and freshly ground black pepper, to taste
- Optional: sesame seeds and sliced green onions for garnish

1. **Prepare Sauce**: Combine soy sauce, oyster sauce, honey, and sesame oil in a bowl.
2. **Heat Griddle**: Set the Blackstone griddle to medium-high (375°F).
3. **Cook Asparagus**: Add 2 tablespoons olive oil and asparagus to the griddle; stir-fry for 3-4 minutes until slightly tender.
4. **Add Shrimp and Seasonings**: Set the asparagus aside. Add the remaining oil, then the shrimp, garlic, and ginger. Season with salt and pepper. Cook for 2-3 minutes until the shrimp are pink.
5. **Combine and Finish**: Pour sauce over shrimp and asparagus. Stir together for 1-2 minutes until well coated and heated through.
6. **Garnish and Serve**: Optionally, sprinkle with sesame seeds and green onions. Serve hot with rice or noodles.

Chicken Fried Rice Stir-Fry

PREP. TIME: 10 min
COOKING TIME: 20 min
SERVES: 4-6

- 4 cups jasmine rice, cooked and chilled
- 2 chicken breasts, cubed
- 1/2 medium onion, diced
- 1 cup mixed vegetables (peas, carrots, green beans)
- 4 eggs
- 3 tablespoons sweet soy sauce

- 2 tablespoons sesame oil
- 1 tablespoon vegetable oil
- 2 cloves garlic, minced
- Sesame seeds, for garnish
- Salt and pepper, to taste (optional)

1. **Prep Ingredients**: Cube chicken, dice onion, and chill cooked jasmine rice in the fridge for 8-10 hours.
2. **Heat Griddle**: Set Blackstone griddle to medium (350°F). Spread vegetable oil on the griddle.
3. **Cook Chicken**: Place the chicken and garlic on the griddle, and cook until golden (about 5-7 minutes). Chop the chicken into smaller pieces during cooking.
4. **Add Vegetables**: Set the chicken aside. Add the vegetables and onion to the griddle, drizzle with sesame oil and soy sauce, and cook until tender.
5. **Prepare Rice**: Combine vegetables with chicken. Add more oil, spread the rice, and season with soy sauce and sesame oil. Mix well.
6. **Cook Eggs**: Clear an area on the griddle, crack eggs onto it, scramble, and then fold into the rice mixture.
7. **Season**: Adjust the seasoning with soy sauce, sesame oil, and salt and pepper, if desired. Garnish with sesame seeds.
8. **Serve**: Once combined and heated through, serve the fried rice directly from the griddle.

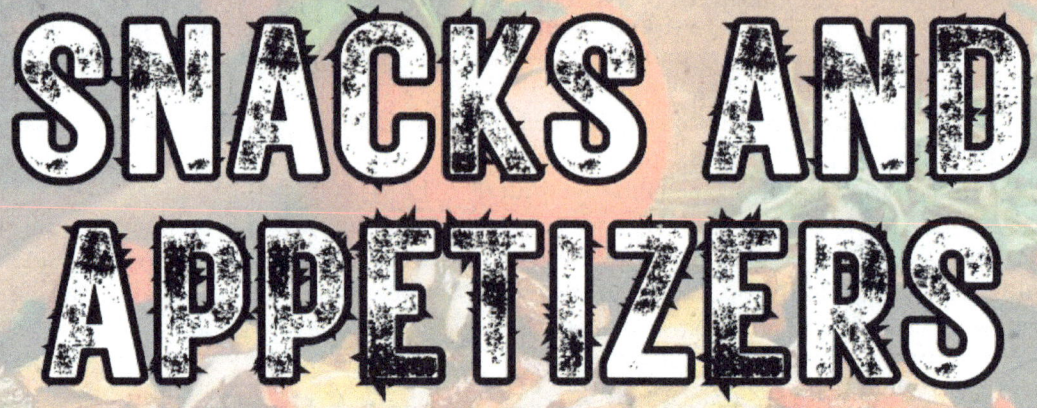

SNACKS AND APPETIZERS

Cheesy Garlic Bread

- 1 large loaf of French bread
- 1/2 cup butter, softened
- 4 cloves garlic, minced
- 2 tablespoons fresh parsley, chopped
- 1 cup shredded mozzarella cheese
- 1/2 cup grated Parmesan cheese
- Salt and pepper, to taste

PREP. TIME: 10 min

COOKING TIME: 5 min

SERVES: 4-6

1. **Prepare Garlic Butter**: In a small bowl, mix the softened butter with minced garlic, chopped parsley, salt, and pepper until well combined.
2. **Prepare the Bread**: Cut the French bread in half lengthwise. Spread the garlic butter evenly over the cut sides of the bread.
3. **Add Cheese**: Sprinkle the shredded mozzarella and grated Parmesan evenly over the buttered surfaces of the bread.
4. **Preheat the Griddle**: Heat your Blackstone gas griddle to medium heat, around 350°F.
5. **Grill the Bread**: Place the bread halves, buttered side down, on the griddle. Cook for about 2-3 minutes or until the bread is golden and toasty and the cheese is melted. Watch carefully to avoid burning.
6. **Serve**: Remove the bread from the griddle. Cut into slices and serve warm as an appetizer or alongside your favorite pasta dish.

Buffalo Chicken Sliders

- 1 pound ground chicken
- 1/4 cup buffalo wing sauce (plus extra for drizzling)
- 1 teaspoon garlic powder
- Salt and pepper, to taste
- 12 slider buns
- 1/2 cup ranch or blue cheese dressing
- 1/2 cup crumbled blue cheese (optional)
- 1 small red onion, thinly sliced
- 1/2 cup celery leaves or thinly sliced celery sticks
- 2 tablespoons vegetable oil

PREP. TIME: 15 min

COOKING TIME: 10 min

SERVES: 4-6

1. **Prepare Chicken Patties**: In a bowl, combine ground chicken with buffalo wing sauce, garlic powder, salt, and pepper. Mix thoroughly. Form the mixture into 12 small patties, slightly larger than the buns to account for shrinkage during cooking.
2. **Preheat the Griddle**: Heat your Blackstone gas griddle to medium-high heat, about 375°F.
3. **Cook Patties**: Brush the griddle with vegetable oil. Place the chicken patties on the griddle and cook for about 4-5 minutes per side, or until fully cooked (internal temperature should reach 165°F) and nicely browned. During the last minute of cooking, optionally top each patty with a small amount of crumbled blue cheese to melt.
4. **Prepare Buns**: Toast the slider buns on the griddle, cut-side down, until golden and crispy, about 1-2 minutes.
5. **Assemble Sliders**: On the bottom half of each bun, spread a generous amount of ranch or blue cheese dressing. Place a cooked chicken patty on each bun, add a drizzle of additional buffalo sauce if desired, then top with red onion slices and celery leaves. Cover with the top half of the bun.
6. **Serve**: Arrange the sliders on a platter and serve immediately, perfect for parties, game days, or a flavorful lunch.

BBQ Chicken Skewers

PREP. TIME: 20 min
COOKING TIME: 10 min
SERVES: 4

- 2 pounds chicken breast, cut into 1-inch cubes
- 1 cup BBQ sauce (plus extra for serving)
- 2 tablespoons olive oil
- 1 tablespoon honey
- 1 teaspoon smoked paprika
- 1 teaspoon garlic powder
- Salt and freshly ground black pepper to taste
- Wooden or metal skewers (if using wooden skewers, soak them in water for at least 30 minutes prior to grilling to prevent burning)

1. **Marinate the Chicken**: In a large bowl, combine the BBQ sauce, olive oil, honey, smoked paprika, and garlic powder. Season with salt and pepper to taste. Add the chicken cubes to the bowl and toss to coat evenly. Cover and refrigerate for at least 1 hour, or overnight for deeper flavor.
2. **Preheat the Griddle**: Heat your Blackstone gas griddle to medium-high heat, around 375°F.
3. **Prepare Skewers**: Thread the marinated chicken pieces onto the skewers, leaving a small space between each piece to ensure even cooking.
4. **Grill the Skewers**: Place the skewers on the hot griddle. Grill for about 4-5 minutes on each side, or until the chicken is well-seared on the outside and reaches an internal temperature of 165°F.
5. **Serve**: Remove the chicken skewers from the griddle and let them rest for a few minutes. Serve with additional BBQ sauce on the side for dipping.
6. **Garnish and Enjoy**: Optionally, garnish with fresh chopped herbs like parsley or cilantro before serving.

Mini Quesadillas

PREP. TIME: 10 min
COOKING TIME: 5 min
SERVES: 4-6

- 12 small flour tortillas (about 6 inches in diameter)
- 2 cups shredded cheese (cheddar, Monterey Jack, or a blend)
- 1 cup cooked chicken, finely chopped or shredded (optional)
- 1/4 cup thinly sliced jalapeños
- 1/2 cup finely chopped onions
- Olive oil or butter for grilling
- Sour cream, salsa, and guacamole for serving
- 1/2 cup diced bell peppers (mix of colors)

1. **Preheat the Griddle**: Heat your Blackstone gas griddle to medium heat, around 350°F.
2. **Assemble Quesadillas**: Lay out half of the tortillas on a clean surface. Sprinkle each with a generous amount of cheese. Add chicken, bell peppers, jalapeños, and onions evenly among the tortillas. Top with the remaining tortillas to form sandwiches.
3. **Cook Quesadillas**: Lightly brush the griddle with olive oil or butter. Place the assembled quesadillas on the griddle. Cook for about 2-3 minutes on each side or until the tortillas are golden brown and the cheese is melted. Use a spatula to flip them carefully to avoid spilling the fillings.
4. **Serve**: Remove the quesadillas from the griddle and let them sit for 1-2 minutes to set. Using a pizza cutter or a sharp knife, cut each quesadilla into quarters. Serve warm with sides of sour cream, salsa, and guacamole.

Loaded Grilled Nachos

PREP. TIME: 10 min
COOKING TIME: 5 min
SERVES: 6

- 1 large bag of tortilla chips
- 2 cups shredded cheddar cheese
- 1 cup shredded Monterey Jack cheese
- 1 cup black beans, rinsed and drained
- 1/2 cup sliced jalapeños
- 1 large tomato, diced
- 1/2 red onion, finely chopped
- 1/4 cup sliced black olives (optional)
- 1/4 cup chopped cilantro
- 1 avocado, diced (for garnish)
- Sour cream for serving
- Salsa, for serving
- Lime wedges, for serving

1. **Heat the Griddle**: Set the Blackstone griddle to medium heat (350°F).
2. **Arrange the Nachos**: Spread tortilla chips in a single layer on the griddle. Sprinkle both types of cheese over the chips.
3. **Add Toppings**: Distribute black beans, jalapeños, tomatoes, onions, and olives over the cheese.
4. **Melt the Cheese**: Cook the nachos on the griddle for 3-5 minutes or until the cheese melts. Cover with a metal bowl or lid to quicken cheese melting and ensure even heating.
5. **Garnish and Serve**: Once cooked, remove nachos from the griddle. Garnish with avocado, cilantro, and lime wedges. Serve with sour cream and salsa.

Cheesesteak Taquitos

- 1 lb ribeye steak, thinly sliced and roughly chopped
- White corn tortillas
- Mixed cheeses (cheddar, smoked three-pepper blend Gouda, hot pepper jack), shredded
- Diced peppers and onions
- Beef tallow for cooking
- Avocado oil
- Garlic Jalapeño seasoning (or similar)
- Cheese sauce for dipping

PREP. TIME: 20 min

COOKING TIME: 15 min

SERVES: 4-6

Prepare the Filling:

1. Preheat your Blackstone griddle to high heat for a good sear on the meat.
2. Place beef tallow on the griddle and add the ribeye slices once it's hot. Cook until they begin to sear.
3. Add diced peppers and onions alongside the meat. Cook until the vegetables are tender and the beef is well-seared.
4. Season the steak and vegetables with garlic Jalapeño seasoning or your choice of spices.

Assemble the Taquitos:

5. Warm the tortillas on the griddle briefly to make them pliable.
6. Lay out the tortillas, and on each, distribute a mix of the cooked steak, peppers, onions, and a generous amount of shredded cheese.
7. Roll the tortillas tightly around the filling, ensuring the seam is on the bottom to prevent them from unrolling during cooking.

Cook the Taquitos:

8. Add a thin layer of avocado oil to the griddle. Place the taquitos seam-side down to seal them shut.
9. Cook, turning occasionally, until all sides are crispy and golden.

Serve:

10. Serve hot with a side of warm cheese sauce for dipping.

Fully Loaded Smash Potatoes

- 4 large Yukon Gold potatoes, pre-boiled
- 6 strips of thick-cut bacon
- 1/2 cup green onions, chopped
- 1 tsp thyme
- 1 tsp onion powder
- 1 tsp paprika
- 1 tsp garlic powder
- 1 tsp Cajun spice (e.g., Kinders Cali Black)
- 4 tbsp butter, melted
- 1 cup mixed cheddar cheese, shredded
- Salt and pepper, to taste
- Avocado oil, for cooking
- Optional: parchment paper for smashing

PREP. TIME: 15 min

COOKING TIME: 25 min

SERVES: 4

1. **Prep the Bacon:** Lay bacon strips on a cold griddle. Turn on the griddle to cook the bacon flat and evenly until crispy. Remove and chop once cooled.
2. **Prepare Butter Sauce:** In a bowl, mix melted butter with thyme, onion powder, paprika, garlic powder, and Cajun spice. Set aside for topping.
3. **Cook the Potatoes:** Heat avocado oil on the griddle over medium heat. Place boiled potatoes on the griddle, smash each gently with a smasher lined with parchment paper to prevent sticking. Cook until the bottoms are golden and crispy for about 5-7 minutes, then flip and cook the other side.
4. **Season and Serve:** Drizzle half of the butter sauce over the crispy potatoes, add the cooked bacon, sprinkle with cheese, and top with green onions. Cover with a dome or another pot lid to melt the cheese for about 1-2 minutes. Finish by drizzling the remaining butter sauce over the cheesy, bacon-topped potatoes.
5. **Garnish and Enjoy:** Serve your fully loaded smash potatoes hot directly from the griddle. Perfect as a hearty camping meal or a satisfying outdoor snack.

PIZZAS RECIPES

Griddle Pizza Margherita

- 1 pound pizza dough (store-bought or homemade)
- 1/2 cup tomato sauce (preferably homemade or high-quality store-bought)
- 8 ounces fresh mozzarella cheese, sliced
- Fresh basil leaves
- Olive oil, for drizzling
- Salt and freshly ground black pepper, to taste
- Extra virgin olive oil, for finishing
- Optional: red pepper flakes

PREP. TIME: 15 min

COOKING TIME: 10 min

SERVES: 2-4

1. **Preheat the Griddle**: Set your Blackstone griddle to medium-high heat, around 400°F.
2. **Prepare the Dough**: Stretch or roll out to about 1/4 inch thick like oven preparation.
3. **Cook the Base**: Lightly oil the griddle. Place dough on the griddle and cook until the bottom is golden about 3-4 minutes. Flip the dough.
4. **Assemble the Pizza**: Quickly spread tomato sauce, arrange mozzarella slices and season. Reduce heat to medium.
5. **Cover and Cook**: Cover the pizza with a metal dome or aluminum foil to melt the cheese and cook the top of the dough for about 5-6 minutes.
6. **Garnish and Serve**: Remove from griddle, garnish with basil, drizzle with olive oil, and optionally sprinkle with red pepper flakes.

BBQ Chicken Griddle Pizza

- 1 pound pizza dough (store-bought or homemade)
- 1/2 cup BBQ sauce, plus extra for drizzling
- 1 cup cooked and shredded chicken
- 1/2 red onion, thinly sliced
- 1 cup shredded smoked gouda cheese
- 1 cup shredded mozzarella cheese
- Fresh cilantro, chopped (for garnish)
- Olive oil, for drizzling

PREP. TIME: 15 min

COOKING TIME: 10min

SERVES: 2-4

1. **Preheat the Griddle**: Set your Blackstone griddle to medium-high heat, around 400°F.
2. **Prepare the Dough**: Stretch or roll the pizza dough to about 1/4 inch thick.
3. **Cook the Base**: Lightly oil the griddle. Place dough on the griddle and cook until the bottom is golden about 3-4 minutes. Flip the dough.
4. **Assemble the Pizza**: Quickly spread BBQ sauce and add shredded chicken, onions, and cheese.
5. **Cover and Cook**: Cover the pizza with a metal dome or aluminum foil to melt the cheese and cook the top of the dough for about 5-7 minutes.
6. **Garnish and Serve**: Remove from griddle, sprinkle with cilantro, and drizzle with more BBQ sauce.

Buffalo Griddle Flatbread

PREP. TIME: 10 min

COOKING TIME: 8 min

SERVES: 2-4

- 1 pre-made pizza crust or flatbread
- 1/2 cup buffalo wing sauce
- 1 cup cooked chicken breast, shredded
- 1/2 cup blue cheese, crumbled
- 1/2 cup mozzarella cheese, shredded
- 1/4 cup celery, thinly sliced
- 1/4 cup red onion, thinly sliced
- 2 tablespoons ranch or blue cheese dressing (for drizzling)
- Fresh parsley, chopped (for garnish)

1. **Preheat the Griddle**: Heat your Blackstone gas griddle to medium heat, around 350°F.
2. **Prepare the Flatbread**: Place the flatbread on the griddle to warm up and start to crisp slightly, about 1-2 minutes per side. Remove and set aside.
3. **Add Sauces and Toppings**: Spread buffalo wing sauce evenly over the warmed flatbread. Sprinkle the shredded chicken over the sauce, followed by the red onion and celery.
4. **Add Cheeses**: Distribute both blue cheese and mozzarella evenly over the toppings.
5. **Cook the Flatbread**: Return the flatbread to the griddle. Cover with a metal dome or aluminum foil to melt the cheese and heat the toppings through, about 5-6 minutes.
6. **Garnish and Serve**: Remove from the griddle once the cheese is melted and the toppings are hot. Drizzle ranch or blue cheese dressing over the top, and garnish with chopped parsley. Cut into pieces and serve warm.

Griddle Pizza Rolls

PREP. TIME: 20 min

COOKING TIME: 10 min

SERVES: 4-6

- 1 pound mild Italian sausage, crumbled
- 1 cup pepperoni, sliced
- 2 cups mozzarella cheese, shredded
- 1 tablespoon Tuscan herb seasoning (or Italian seasoning)
- 4 large flour tortillas
- 1/2 cup marinara sauce (Rayo's Tomato Basil or similar)
- Additional toppings as desired (e.g., onions, mushrooms, bell peppers, jalapeños)
- Olive oil for griddling

1. **Preheat the Griddle**: Heat your Blackstone gas griddle to medium heat, around 350°F.
2. **Cook the Sausage**: Place the crumbled Italian sausage on the griddle. Cook until browned and fully cooked through, about 5-7 minutes. Move to one side of the griddle.
3. **Toast the Pepperoni**: Lay out pepperoni slices in another area of the griddle. Toast them slightly on each side for 1-2 minutes, then move them to the sausage.
4. **Assemble the Pizza Rolls**: Lay out the flour tortillas on the griddle. Sprinkle mozzarella cheese evenly over each tortilla. Add cooked sausage and toasted pepperoni, and sprinkle with Tuscan herb seasoning. Allow the cheese to start melting.
5. **Roll and Cook**: Once the cheese melts, roll the tortillas tightly around the fillings on the griddle to form a sealed roll. Press slightly with a spatula to ensure they hold together.
6. **Finish Cooking**: Allow the rolls to crisp up on the outside, turning once to ensure even cooking and browning, about 2-3 minutes per side.
7. **Serve**: Slice the rolls into sections. Serve with marinara sauce spooned over the top or on the side for dipping.

Tortilla Pizza

PREP. TIME: 10 min

COOKING TIME: 10 min

SERVES: 2-4

- 2 large flour tortillas
- Butter for spreading on tortillas
- 1/2 cup pizza sauce
- 1 cup freshly shredded mozzarella cheese, divided
- 1/2 cup mini pepperonis
- 1 cooked hamburger patty, crumbled
- 2 slices of bacon, cooked and chopped
- Optional toppings: onion, green chilies

1. **Preheat the Griddle**: Set your Blackstone gas griddle to low heat to ensure it cooks without burning the tortillas.
2. **Prepare the Tortillas**: Butter one side of each tortilla. Place one tortilla, buttered side down, on the griddle. Quickly sprinkle a layer of cheese over this tortilla.
3. **Create Stuffed Base**: Place the second tortilla on top of the first, buttered side up. This double layer will create a sturdy base for your toppings. Allow the tortillas to crisp slightly for about 2 minutes, ensuring they are golden but not burnt.
4. **Add Sauce and Toppings**: Spread pizza sauce over the top tortilla. Add another layer of shredded mozzarella cheese, then evenly distribute the pepperoni, crumbled hamburger, and bacon over the cheese. If using additional toppings like onions or green chilies, add them now.
5. **Cook the Pizza**: Cover the pizza with a dome or aluminum foil to melt the cheese and heat the toppings thoroughly. Optionally, squirt a little water under the dome to create steam, which helps melt the cheese without making the tortillas soggy.
6. **Finish and Serve**: After the cheese has melted and the bottom tortilla is crispy (about 2-3 minutes), check the bottom of the pizza to ensure it is perfectly cooked. Remove the pizza from the griddle, cut into slices, and serve hot.

SAUCES AND RUBS

Classic BBQ Sauce (Meat)

PREP. TIME: 10 min
COOKING TIME: 20-25 min
SERVES: 2 cups

- 1 cup tomato ketchup
- 1/2 cup apple cider vinegar
- 1/2 cup brown sugar
- 1/4 cup honey
- 2 tablespoons Worcestershire sauce
- 1 tablespoon smoked paprika
- 1 teaspoon garlic powder
- 1 teaspoon onion powder
- 1/2 teaspoon ground mustard
- 1/4 teaspoon cayenne pepper (adjust based on heat preference)
- Salt and black pepper to taste

1. **Combine Ingredients**: In a medium saucepan, combine the ketchup, apple cider vinegar, brown sugar, and honey. Stir together over medium heat until the sugar begins to dissolve.
2. **Add Spices**: Mix in the Worcestershire sauce, smoked paprika, garlic powder, onion powder, ground mustard, and cayenne pepper. Stir well to ensure all ingredients are fully integrated.
3. **Simmer**: Bring the mixture to a simmer. Reduce the heat to low and let it cook for about 20-25 minutes, stirring occasionally. The sauce should thicken slightly as it simmers.
4. **Season**: Taste the sauce and adjust the seasoning with salt and black pepper. If you desire more sweetness or acidity, you can add more honey or vinegar to taste.
5. **Cool and Store**: Remove the sauce from heat and allow it to cool to room temperature. Once cooled, transfer the BBQ sauce to an airtight container or jar and refrigerate.
6. **Serve**: Use this Classic BBQ Sauce for grilling, marinating meats like chicken, pork, or beef, or as a tasty dipping sauce. Its rich, smoky, and slightly spicy taste will enhance the flavor of your meals.

This BBQ sauce can be stored in the refrigerator for up to 2 weeks. Before using, stir it well, as some separation might occur. Enjoy your homemade sauce with your favorite grilled dishes!

Spicy Chipotle BBQ Sauce (Meat)

PREP. TIME: 20 min
COOKING TIME: 10 min
SERVES: 2 cups

- 1 cup tomato sauce
- 1/2 cup apple cider vinegar
- 1/3 cup brown sugar
- 3 tablespoons honey
- 2 chipotle peppers in adobo sauce, finely chopped
- 2 tablespoons adobo sauce (from the chipotle peppers can)
- 1 tablespoon smoked paprika
- 1 teaspoon garlic powder
- 1 teaspoon onion powder
- 1/2 teaspoon ground cumin
- Salt and pepper to taste

1. **Combine Ingredients**: In a medium saucepan, combine the tomato sauce, apple cider vinegar, brown sugar, and honey. Stir together over medium heat until the sugar begins to dissolve.
2. **Add Spices and Peppers**: Mix in the chipotle peppers, adobo sauce, smoked paprika, garlic powder, onion powder, and ground cumin. Stir well to ensure all ingredients are fully integrated.
3. **Simmer**: Bring the mixture to a simmer. Reduce the heat to low and let it cook for about 20-25 minutes, stirring occasionally. The sauce should thicken slightly as it simmers.
4. **Season**: Taste the sauce and adjust the seasoning with salt and pepper. If you desire more heat, you can add more chopped chipotle peppers or a dash of cayenne pepper.
5. **Blend (Optional):** Use an immersion blender to puree the sauce directly in the pan until it reaches your desired consistency for a smoother sauce. Alternatively, you can transfer the sauce to a blender, blend until smooth, and then return it to the pan.
6. **Cool and Store**: Allow the sauce to cool completely. Once cooled, transfer it to an airtight container and refrigerate. The sauce will develop more flavor as it sits and can be stored in the refrigerator for up to 2 weeks.
7. **Serve**: Use your Spicy Chipotle BBQ Sauce as a marinade for meats, a basting sauce for grilling, or as a flavorful addition to sandwiches and burgers.

This rich and spicy BBQ sauce is perfect for those who love a deep, smoky flavor with a bit of heat. It's ideal for enhancing the taste of any grilled meat or adding an extra zing to your barbecue meals.

Herb Garlic Marinade Recipe (Meat)

PREP. TIME: 10 min
COOKING TIME: -
SERVES:

- 1/2 cup olive oil
- 4 cloves garlic, minced
- 2 tablespoons fresh rosemary, finely chopped
- 2 tablespoons fresh thyme, finely chopped
- 2 tablespoons fresh parsley, finely chopped
- Zest of 1 lemon
- Juice of 1 lemon
- 1 teaspoon salt
- 1/2 teaspoon black pepper

1. **Combine Ingredients**: In a medium mixing bowl, combine the olive oil, minced garlic, chopped rosemary, chopped thyme, chopped parsley, lemon zest, lemon juice, salt, and black pepper.
2. **Mix Well**: Whisk the ingredients together until well combined. The marinade should have a uniform consistency, with the herbs evenly distributed.
3. **Marinate the Meat**: Place your choice of meat (such as steaks, lamb chops, or chicken) in a large, resealable plastic bag or a shallow dish. Pour the marinade over the meat, ensuring it is well coated. Seal the bag or cover the dish.
4. **Refrigerate**: For best results, let the meat marinate in the refrigerator for at least 2 hours or overnight. Turn the meat occasionally to ensure even marination.
5. **Grill**: Preheat your Blackstone griddle to medium-high heat. Remove the meat from the marinade, allowing any excess to drip off. Grill the meat to your desired doneness, typically 4-6 minutes per side for steaks, depending on thickness.
6. **Serve**: Once cooked, let the meat rest for a few minutes before serving to allow the juices to redistribute. Enjoy your flavorful, herb-infused grilled meat!

This Herb Garlic Marinade imparts a fresh and aromatic flavor to meats, perfect for grilling on your Blackstone griddle. The combination of herbs, garlic, and lemon makes it a versatile and delicious marinade for any occasion.

Bourbon Whiskey Glaze (Meat)

PREP. TIME: 10 min
COOKING TIME: 15-20 min
SERVES: 1 cups

- 1/2 cup bourbon whiskey
- 1/2 cup brown sugar
- 1/4 cup ketchup
- 1/4 cup apple cider vinegar
- 2 tablespoons Worcestershire sauce
- 1 tablespoon Dijon mustard
- 1 tablespoon soy sauce
- 1 teaspoon minced garlic
- 1 teaspoon minced ginger (optional)
- 1/4 teaspoon black pepper
- Pinch of cayenne pepper (optional)

1. **Combine Ingredients**: In a medium saucepan, combine the bourbon whiskey, brown sugar, ketchup, apple cider vinegar, Worcestershire sauce, Dijon mustard, soy sauce, minced garlic, and minced ginger (if using).
2. **Mix Well**: Stir the ingredients together over medium heat until the sugar is fully dissolved and the mixture is well combined.
3. **Simmer**: Bring the mixture to a simmer. Reduce the heat to low and let it cook for about 15-20 minutes, stirring occasionally, until the glaze thickens to your desired consistency.
4. **Season**: Add black pepper and a pinch of cayenne pepper (if using) to taste. Stir well to incorporate the spices.
5. **Cool and Store**: Remove the glaze from heat and let it cool to room temperature. Once cooled, transfer it to an airtight container or jar. The glaze can be stored in the refrigerator for up to 2 weeks.
6. **Serve**: Use this Bourbon Whiskey Glaze to brush on grilled meats like chicken wings, pork chops, or beef steaks during the last few minutes of grilling. It can also be used as a flavorful dipping sauce.

This Bourbon Whiskey Glaze adds a rich, sweet, and tangy flavor with a hint of smokiness to your grilled dishes, making it a perfect complement for any barbecue. Enjoy the deliciously glazed meats with your favorite sides!

Lemon Dill Sauce (Fish)

PREP. TIME: 10 min
COOKING TIME: -
SERVES: 1 cup

- 1 cup sour cream or Greek yogurt
- 2 tablespoons fresh dill, finely chopped
- 1 tablespoon lemon zest
- 2 tablespoons lemon juice
- 1 clove garlic, minced
- Salt and black pepper to taste

1. **Combine Ingredients**: In a medium mixing bowl, combine the sour cream or Greek yogurt, finely chopped dill, lemon zest, lemon juice, and minced garlic.
2. **Mix Well**: Stir the ingredients together until well combined. Ensure the dill and garlic are evenly distributed throughout the sauce.
3. **Season**: Add salt and black pepper to taste. Stir well to incorporate the seasonings.
4. **Chill**: Cover the bowl with plastic wrap and refrigerate for at least 30 minutes to allow the flavors to meld together. This step enhances the taste of the sauce.
5. **Serve**: The Lemon Dill Sauce can be chilled and served as a topping for grilled fish such as salmon or trout or as a dipping sauce for grilled vegetables.

This Lemon Dill Sauce provides a fresh, creamy, and tangy flavor, perfect for enhancing the taste of your grilled dishes. Enjoy the bright and zesty notes with your favorite meals!

Cajun Spice Rub (Fish)

PREP. TIME: 5 min
COOKING TIME: -
SERVES: 1/2 cups

- 2 tablespoons paprika
- 1 tablespoon garlic powder
- 1 tablespoon onion powder
- 1 tablespoon dried oregano
- 1 tablespoon dried thyme
- 1 tablespoon cayenne pepper (adjust to taste)
- 1 tablespoon black pepper
- 1 tablespoon white pepper
- 1 tablespoon salt

1. **Combine Ingredients**: In a small bowl, combine the paprika, garlic powder, onion powder, dried oregano, dried thyme, cayenne pepper, black pepper, white pepper, and salt.
2. **Mix Well**: Stir the ingredients together until they are evenly mixed and no clumps remain.
3. **Store**: Transfer the Cajun Spice Rub to an airtight container or jar. It can be stored in a cool, dry place for up to 6 months.
4. **Use**: Generously rub the spice mixture onto meats, fish, or vegetables before grilling. Ensure that the surface of the food is evenly coated with the rub.

This Cajun Spice Rub brings a robust and spicy flavor to your grilled dishes, making it perfect for seasoning shrimp, chicken, fish, or vegetables before cooking on your Blackstone griddle. Enjoy the bold and zesty taste of Cajun cuisine!

Balsamic Herb Vinaigrette (Vegetables)

PREP. TIME: 10 min

COOKING TIME: -

SERVES: 3/4 cup

- 1/4 cup balsamic vinegar
- 1/2 cup extra-virgin olive oil
- 1 tablespoon Dijon mustard
- 1 clove garlic, minced
- 1 teaspoon honey or maple syrup
- 1 tablespoon fresh basil, finely chopped
- 1 tablespoon fresh oregano, finely chopped
- Salt and black pepper to taste

1. **Combine Vinegar and Mustard:** In a medium mixing bowl, whisk together the balsamic vinegar and Dijon mustard until well combined.
2. **Add Garlic and Sweetener:** Stir in the minced garlic and honey (or maple syrup) until fully incorporated.
3. **Add Herbs:** Mix in the finely chopped basil and oregano.
4. **Emulsify:** Slowly drizzle in the extra-virgin olive oil while continuously whisking to emulsify the vinaigrette. This will create a smooth and well-blended dressing.
5. **Season:** Add salt and black pepper to taste, adjusting as needed.
6. **Store:** Transfer the vinaigrette to an airtight container or jar. It can be stored in the refrigerator for up to 1 week. Shake well before each use.
7. **Serve:** Drizzle the Balsamic Herb Vinaigrette over grilled vegetables and mixed greens, or use it as a marinade for grilled chicken or fish.

This Balsamic Herb Vinaigrette offers a perfect balance of tangy, sweet, and herbaceous flavors, making it an excellent addition to your grilled dishes. Enjoy the fresh and vibrant taste with your favorite vegetables and proteins!

Smoky Chipotle Lime Dressing (Vegetables)

PREP. TIME: 10 min

COOKING TIME: -

SERVES: 3/4 cup

- 2 chipotle peppers in adobo sauce, finely chopped
- 1/4 cup lime juice (about 2-3 limes)
- 1/2 cup olive oil
- 2 tablespoons honey
- 1/4 cup fresh cilantro, finely chopped
- Salt and black pepper to taste

1. **Combine Lime Juice and Honey:** In a medium mixing bowl, whisk together the lime juice and honey until the honey is fully dissolved.
2. **Add Chipotle and Cilantro:** Stir in the finely chopped chipotle peppers and adobo sauce, and the finely chopped cilantro. Mix well to combine.
3. **Emulsify:** Slowly drizzle in the olive oil while continuously whisking to emulsify the dressing. This will create a smooth and well-blended mixture.
4. **Season:** Add salt and black pepper to taste, adjusting as needed.
5. **Store:** Transfer the Smoky Chipotle Lime Dressing to an airtight container or jar. It can be stored in the refrigerator for up to 1 week. Shake well before each use.
6. **Serve:** Drizzle the Smoky Chipotle Lime Dressing over grilled corn on the cob, mixed grilled vegetable platters, or use it as a zesty marinade for grilled chicken or fish.

This Smoky Chipotle Lime Dressing combines the smoky heat of chipotle with the bright tang of lime, balanced by a touch of sweetness from the honey. It's perfect for adding a flavorful kick to your grilled vegetables and other favorite dishes.

SPECIAL OCCASIONS

BBQ Ribs (Memorial Day)

- 2 racks of pork ribs (about 4-6 lbs)
- 1/4 cup brown sugar
- 1 tablespoon paprika
- 1 tablespoon garlic powder
- 1 tablespoon onion powder
- 1 teaspoon cayenne pepper (optional for heat)
- Salt and black pepper to taste
- 1 cup barbecue sauce

PREP. TIME: 15 min

COOKING TIME: 2-3 h

SERVES: 4-6

1. **Prepare the Ribs**: Remove the membrane and pat dry. Mix brown sugar, paprika, garlic powder, onion powder, cayenne, salt, and pepper. Generously season both sides of the ribs.
2. **Preheat the Griddle**: Set the Blackstone Griddle to maintain a steady low heat of 225°F.
3. **Cook the Ribs**: Place the ribs bone-side down, cover with foil or close the lid, and cook for 2-3 hours until tender.
4. **Glaze the Ribs**: In the final 30 minutes, brush with barbecue sauce, turning and basting frequently to build up a rich glaze.
5. **Rest and Serve**: Once cooked, let the ribs rest for 10 minutes before slicing. Serve with extra barbecue sauce and sides like coleslaw and cornbread.

Grilled Bratwurst with Sauerkraut (Independence Day)

- 6 bratwurst sausages
- 3 cups sauerkraut, drained
- 6 hoagie rolls or hot dog buns
- Mustard, for serving
- 1 onion, thinly sliced (optional)
- Olive oil for grilling

PREP. TIME: 20 min

COOKING TIME: 10 min

SERVES: 4-6

1. **Preheat the Griddle**: Heat your Blackstone gas griddle to medium heat, around 350°F.
2. **Grill the Bratwurst**: Place the bratwurst sausages on the griddle. Grill them until they are browned and fully cooked through, about 5-7 minutes per side, turning occasionally to ensure even cooking.
3. **Sauté the Onions**: If using onions, add a little olive oil to another area of the griddle. Add the sliced onions and cook until they are caramelized, stirring frequently for about 5-7 minutes.
4. **Warm the Sauerkraut**: Place the drained sauerkraut on the griddle next to the bratwurst. Let it warm through and slightly caramelize, stirring occasionally for about 3-4 minutes.
5. **Toast the Buns**: Brush the inside of the hoagie rolls or hot dog buns with a light coat of olive oil. Place them cut-side down on the griddle to toast lightly, about 1-2 minutes.
6. **Assemble the Bratwurst**: Place a grilled bratwurst in each toasted bun. Top with warm sauerkraut, caramelized onions (if used), and a generous squirt of mustard.
7. **Serve**: Serve the bratwurst immediately while hot. Optional: accompanied with side dishes such as potato salad or coleslaw for a complete Independence Day meal.

Grilled Veggie Kabobs (Labor Day)

PREP. TIME: 20 min
COOKING TIME: 10-15 min.
SERVES: 4-6

- 2 bell peppers (one red, one yellow), cut into 1-inch pieces
- 2 zucchinis, sliced into 1/2-inch rounds
- 1 large red onion, cut into chunks
- 1 pint cherry tomatoes
- 1 cup whole button mushrooms
- 1/4 cup olive oil
- 2 tablespoons balsamic vinegar
- 2 cloves garlic, minced
- 1 teaspoon dried Italian herbs
- Salt and pepper to taste
- Wooden or metal skewers (if using wooden, soak in water for at least 30 minutes prior to grilling)

1. **Marinate the Vegetables**: In a large bowl, whisk together olive oil, balsamic vinegar, minced garlic, Italian herbs, salt, and pepper. Add the chopped vegetables to the bowl and toss until well coated. Let marinate for at least 15 minutes or up to 2 hours in the refrigerator for more flavor.
2. **Preheat the Griddle**: Heat your Blackstone gas griddle to medium-high heat, around 375°F.
3. **Assemble the Kabobs**: Thread the marinated vegetables onto the skewers, alternating types of vegetables for color and variety.
4. **Grill the Kabobs**: Place the veggie kabobs on the hot griddle. Grill for about 10-15 minutes, turning occasionally, until the vegetables are tender and have nice grill marks.
5. **Serve**: Remove the kabobs from the griddle and serve immediately. Optional: Drizzle with a little extra virgin olive oil or a squeeze of fresh lemon juice before serving for added flavor.

Grilled Lime Cilantro Shrimp Skewers (Summer Weekends)

PREP. TIME: 15 min
COOKING TIME: 20 min.
SERVES: 4-6

- 2 pounds large shrimp, peeled and deveined
- 3 tablespoons olive oil
- Juice and zest of 2 limes
- 2 cloves garlic, minced
- 1/4 cup chopped fresh cilantro
- Salt and pepper to taste

1. **Marinate the Shrimp**: In a large bowl, whisk together olive oil, lime juice, lime zest, minced garlic, chopped cilantro, salt, and pepper. Add the shrimp and toss until well-coated. Cover and refrigerate to marinate for about 20 minutes, ensuring the shrimp are fully flavored.
2. **Preheat the Griddle**: Heat your Blackstone griddle to medium-high heat, ensuring it reaches about 375°F (190°C).
3. **Assemble the Skewers**: Thread the marinated shrimp onto skewers, spacing them evenly.
4. **Grill the Skewers**: Place the shrimp skewers on the hot griddle. Grill for about 3-4 minutes on each side or until the shrimp are opaque and slightly charred on the edges.
5. **Serve**: Remove the skewers from the griddle and serve immediately. Optional: Garnish with additional chopped cilantro and lime wedges for an extra burst of flavor.

Buffalo Chicken Dip (Fall Tailgating)

PREP. TIME: 10 min
COOKING TIME: 20 min
SERVES: 6-8

- 2 cups cooked chicken, shredded
- 1 package (8 oz) cream cheese, softened
- 1/2 cup Buffalo hot sauce
- 1/2 cup ranch or blue cheese dressing
- 1/2 cup crumbled blue cheese (optional; can use extra shredded mozzarella or cheddar cheese)
- 1/2 cup shredded mozzarella cheese
- 2 green onions, sliced (for garnish)
- Celery sticks and tortilla chips for serving

1. **Preheat the Griddle**: Set your Blackstone griddle to medium heat, around 350°F (175°C).
2. **Combine Ingredients**: In a large bowl, mix the shredded chicken with cream cheese, Buffalo hot sauce, ranch or blue cheese dressing, and crumbled blue cheese (if using). Stir until all ingredients are well combined.
3. **Cook the Dip**: Transfer the chicken mixture to a cast iron skillet or a heavy-duty foil pan. Smooth the top with a spatula. Sprinkle the shredded mozzarella cheese evenly over the surface.
4. **Grill the Dip**: Place the skillet or foil pan on the preheated griddle. Close the griddle lid or cover the dip with aluminum foil. Let the dip cook for about 15-20 minutes or until the cheese is bubbly and slightly golden.
5. **Garnish and Serve**: Remove the dip from the griddle and sprinkle sliced green onions on top for garnish. Serve hot with celery sticks and tortilla chips for dipping.

INTERNATIONAL RECIPES

Korean Bulgogi (Asian Style)

- 1 ½ pounds ribeye steak, thinly sliced
- ½ cup soy sauce
- 2 tablespoons sesame oil
- 3 tablespoons brown sugar
- 4 cloves garlic, minced
- 1 medium pear, grated
- 2 green onions, finely chopped
- 1 tablespoon ginger, grated
- 2 tablespoons sesame seeds
- 1 teaspoon black pepper

PREP. TIME: 20 min

COOKING TIME: 10 min (1 h or overnight marinating time for best result)

SERVES: 4

1. **Marinate the Beef**: In a large mixing bowl, combine soy sauce, sesame oil, brown sugar, minced garlic, grated pear, chopped green onions, grated ginger, sesame seeds, and black pepper. Whisk these ingredients together to form the marinade. Add the thinly sliced ribeye steak to the bowl, ensuring each piece is well-coated with the marinade. Cover and refrigerate for at least 1 hour, though overnight marinating is recommended for deeper flavor.
2. **Preheat** Your Blackstone Griddle: Heat your Blackstone griddle to 375°F (190°C). This high temperature is ideal for quickly searing the meat without overcooking it.
3. **Cook the Bulgogi**: Remove the marinated beef from the refrigerator and let it come to room temperature. Spread the beef in a single layer on the hot griddle, discarding any excess marinade. Cook for about 3-5 minutes per side or until the edges are slightly caramelized and the meat is cooked through.
4. **Serve**: Transfer the cooked bulgogi to a serving plate. Sprinkle with additional sesame seeds and green onions if desired. Serve with steamed rice and Korean side dishes like kimchi for a complete meal.

Steak and Shrimp Hibachi (Asian Style)

- 1 pound ribeye steak, sliced
- 1 pound Argentine red shrimp, peeled and deveined
- 2 cups cooked rice
- 2 whole eggs
- 1 cup mixed vegetables (onions, mushrooms, zucchini)
- 4 tablespoons soy sauce
- 2 tablespoons garlic, minced
- 4 tablespoons unsalted butter
- Salt and pepper to taste
- Olive oil for cooking
- 1 lemon, juiced
- 1 lime, juiced
- Optional garnishes: sesame seeds, green onions

PREP. TIME: 15 min

COOKING TIME: 20 min

SERVES: 4

1. **Preheat the Griddle**: Set your Blackstone griddle to medium-high heat, around 375°F (190°C). Ensure it's hot enough for a quick sear.
2. **Prepare the Fried Rice**: Heat oil on the griddle. Scramble eggs until fully cooked and set aside. Add more oil, sauté garlic briefly, and then add the rice. Fry until slightly charred, then mix in the eggs. Season with salt and a bit of soy sauce for color. Keep warm on the side.
3. **Cook the Vegetables**: Add vegetables to the griddle with some oil. Char all sides, season with salt and pepper, and add butter and a splash of soy sauce for flavor. Remove and keep warm once cooked.
4. **Cook the Steak and Shrimp:** Season the steak and shrimp with salt and pepper, and cook in a little oil until the shrimp are pink and opaque and the steak is medium rare, about 3-5 minutes per side, depending on thickness.
5. **Finish:** add butter, garlic, and lemon juice to the steak and lime juice to the shrimp for enhanced flavor.
6. **Serve**: Plate the fried rice, vegetables, steak, and shrimp. Optionally garnish with sesame seeds and green onions.

Italian Sausage and Peppers (Italian Style)

- 1.5 pounds Italian sausage links
- 2 bell peppers, sliced (mix of red and green)
- 1 large onion, sliced
- 2 tablespoons olive oil
- Salt and pepper to taste
- 1 teaspoon Italian seasoning
- 1/4 cup white wine or water (optional, for deglazing)

PREP. TIME: 10 min

COOKING TIME: 15 min

SERVES: 4-6

1. **Preheat the Griddle**: Set your Blackstone griddle to medium heat, around 350°F (175°C).
2. **Cook the Sausages**: Place the Italian sausages on the griddle. Cook until browned on all sides and cooked through about 10-12 minutes. Turn occasionally to ensure even cooking.
3. **Sauté Vegetables**: Add olive oil to another part of the griddle while cooking sausages. Add the sliced peppers and onions and season with salt, pepper, and Italian seasoning. Sauté until vegetables are soft and caramelized, about 7-10 minutes.
4. **Combine and Simmer**: Once sausages are cooked, slice them into bite-sized pieces if preferred, and mix with the sautéed peppers and onions. If using, deglaze the griddle with white wine or water, scraping up any browned bits for added flavor.
5. **Finish and Serve**: Allow the mixture to simmer for 2-3 minutes to blend the flavors. Serve hot, ideal for piling onto hoagie rolls or as a hearty stand-alone dish.

Steak Tortellini (Italian Style)

- 2 sirloin steaks, thinly sliced and chopped into bite-sized pieces
- 1 package pre-cooked tortellini (choose your favorite variety)
- 1 zucchini, sliced
- 1 sweet onion, sliced
- 1 cup cherry tomatoes, halved
- 2 tablespoons olive oil
- 2 tablespoons avocado oil
- 1 tablespoon butter
- Salt and pepper to taste
- Buttery steakhouse seasoning (or salt and pepper to taste)
- 1 cup fresh spinach
- 1/2 cup garlic herb goat cheese
- Water for steaming

PREP. TIME: 15 min

COOKING TIME: 20 min

SERVES: 4-6

1. **Preheat the Griddle**: Set your Blackstone griddle to medium-high heat, around 375°F (190°C).
2. **Prepare the Vegetables**: Drizzle olive and avocado oils on the griddle. Add zucchini, sweet onion, and cherry tomatoes. Season with salt, pepper, and a dab of butter. Cook until they begin to caramelize, about 5-7 minutes.
3. **Cook the Steak**: Place the seasoned steak pieces on the griddle. Season with buttery steakhouse seasoning. Cook until nicely browned and cooked through, about 3-5 minutes per side. Move to one side of the griddle to keep warm.
4. **Steam the Tortellini**: Place the tortellini on the griddle. Add a splash of water and cover with a dome to steam for 2-3 minutes until warmed through.
5. **Combine Ingredients**: Remove the dome and add spinach and garlic herb goat cheese dollops over the tortellini. The cheese will melt and mix gently, incorporating the vegetables and steak.
6. **Finish and Serve**: Once the cheese has melted and coated the ingredients, creating a creamy sauce, remove from heat. Serve the steak tortellini hot, ensuring each plate is filled with a mix of meat, vegetables, and cheesy tortellini.

Jamaican Jerk Chicken Skewers (Caribbean Style)

- 2 pounds chicken breast, cut into 1-inch cubes
- 1/4 cup soy sauce
- 2 tablespoons vegetable oil
- 2 tablespoons vinegar
- Juice of 1 lime
- 3 tablespoons brown sugar
- 1 teaspoon ground allspice
- 1/2 teaspoon nutmeg
- 1/2 teaspoon cinnamon
- 2 teaspoons thyme
- 1 teaspoon ground ginger
- 2 cloves garlic, minced
- 1 Scotch bonnet pepper, finely chopped (adjust to taste)
- Salt and pepper to taste
- Wooden or metal skewers (if using wooden, soak in water for at least 30 minutes prior to use)

PREP. TIME: 20 min (plus marinating time)

COOKING TIME: 15 min

SERVES: 4-6

1. **Marinate the Chicken**: In a large mixing bowl, combine soy sauce, vegetable oil, vinegar, lime juice, brown sugar, allspice, nutmeg, cinnamon, thyme, ginger, garlic, and Scotch bonnet pepper. Whisk together to form the marinade. Season with salt and pepper. Add the chicken pieces to the marinade, ensuring each piece is well-coated. Cover and refrigerate for at least 2 hours, preferably overnight, to infuse flavors.
2. **Preheat Your Blackstone Griddle**: Heat your Blackstone griddle to medium-high heat, around 375°F (190°C). This temperature is ideal for grilling skewers.
3. **Prepare the Skewers**: Thread the marinated chicken pieces onto the skewers, leaving a little space between each piece to ensure even cooking.
4. **Grill the Chicken**: Place the skewers on the hot griddle. Grill for about 6-8 minutes on each side, or until the chicken is golden brown on the outside and cooked through.
5. **Serve**: Remove the chicken skewers from the griddle and let them rest for a few minutes. Serve hot, garnished with lime wedges or alongside a fresh salad or grilled vegetables.

Mexican Street Corn - Elote (Caribbean Style)

- 4 ears of corn, husks removed
- 1/4 cup mayonnaise
- 1/4 cup sour cream or Mexican crema
- 1/2 cup Cotija cheese, crumbled
- 1/2 teaspoon chili powder
- 1/4 teaspoon garlic powder
- 1 lime, cut into wedges
- Chopped cilantro, for garnish
- Salt to taste

PREP. TIME: 10 min

COOKING TIME: 10 min

SERVES: 4

1. **Preheat Your Blackstone Griddle**: Set your Blackstone griddle to medium-high heat, around 375°F (190°C). Ensure it is hot before placing the corn on the griddle.
2. **Grill the Corn**: Place the corn directly on the griddle. Grill the corn, turning occasionally, until it is cooked through and has char marks all around, approximately 8-10 minutes.
3. **Mix Toppings**: While the corn is grilling, mix together the mayonnaise, sour cream, chili powder, garlic powder, and a pinch of salt in a small bowl.
4. **Coat the Corn**: Once the corn is grilled, brush each ear with the mayonnaise mixture, ensuring it is evenly coated.
5. **Add Cheese and Seasonings**: Sprinkle the crumbled Cotija cheese over each corn ear, followed by a light dusting of additional chili powder. If desired, add more salt to taste.
6. **Garnish and Serve**: Garnish with chopped cilantro and serve with lime wedges on the side. Squeeze the lime over the corn before eating for an added zesty flavor.

French Crepes (European Style)

- 1 cup all-purpose flour
- 2 eggs
- 1/2 cup milk
- 1/2 cup water
- 1/4 teaspoon salt
- 2 tablespoons melted butter, plus extra for greasing the griddle
- Optional fillings: sugar, Nutella, jam, fresh fruit, whipped cream, or savory fillings like ham and cheese

PREP. TIME: 10 min

COOKING TIME: 20 min

SERVES: 4-6

1. **Make the Crepe Batter**: Whisk together the flour and eggs in a large mixing bowl. Gradually add in the milk and water, stirring to combine. Add the salt and melted butter, and beat until smooth.
2. **Heat the Blackstone Griddle**: Preheat your Blackstone griddle to medium heat, around 325°F (163°C). Lightly grease the surface with butter to prevent sticking.
3. **Cook the Crepes**: Pour or scoop about 1/4 cup of batter onto the griddle for each crepe. Tilt the griddle in a circular motion so that the batter coats the surface evenly in a thin layer.
4. **Cook Until Golden**: Cook the crepe for about 1-2 minutes until the bottom is light golden brown. Loosen with a spatula, turn, and cook the other side for about 1 minute. Remove the crepe and repeat with the remaining batter.
5. **Fill and Serve**: Fill the crepes with your choice of sweet or savory fillings. Fold the crepes in quarters or roll them up. Serve hot.

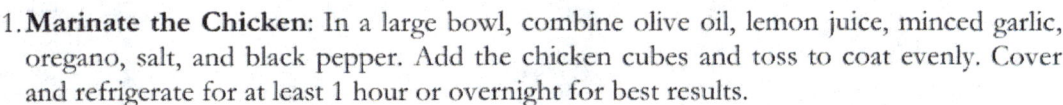

Greek Chicken Souvlaki (European Style)

- 1 1/2 pounds chicken breast, cut into 1-inch cubes
- 3 tablespoons olive oil
- Juice of 1 lemon
- 3 cloves garlic, minced
- 2 teaspoons dried oregano
- 1/2 teaspoon salt
- 1/4 teaspoon black pepper

- 1 red onion, cut into 1-inch pieces
- Optional: bell peppers, cut into 1-inch pieces
- Wooden or metal skewers (if using wooden skewers, soak in water for 30 minutes prior to grilling)
- Fresh parsley, chopped, for garnish
- Lemon wedges, for serving

PREP. TIME: 15 min (plus marinating time)
COOKING TIME: 10 min

SERVES: 4

1. **Marinate the Chicken**: In a large bowl, combine olive oil, lemon juice, minced garlic, oregano, salt, and black pepper. Add the chicken cubes and toss to coat evenly. Cover and refrigerate for at least 1 hour or overnight for best results.
2. **Preheat Your Blackstone Griddle**: Heat your Blackstone griddle to medium-high heat, around 375°F (190°C).
3. **Prepare the Skewers**: Thread the marinated chicken and pieces of red onion (and bell peppers if using) onto the skewers.
4. **Grill the Souvlaki**: Place the skewers on the hot griddle. Grill for about 10 minutes, turning occasionally, until the chicken is golden brown and cooked through.
5. **Serve**: Garnish the chicken souvlaki with chopped fresh parsley and serve with lemon wedges on the side.

SCAN THE QR CODE
AND
GET YOUR BONUSES
NOW!

D	TEMPERATURE
	325 - 375 °F
adian Bacon	250 - 280 °F
s, Fried	325 - 375 °F
Fish	325 - 350 °F
rench Toast	325 - 350 °F
am (Ham Steak)	350 - 375 °F
Hamburger	350 - 375 °F
Hash Browns	325 - 375 °F
Pancakes	325 - 375 °F
Pork Chops	300 - 350 °F
Potatoes	325 - 375 °F
Sausage (link, patty)	325 - 375 °F
Sandwiches (grilled bread)	200 - 250 °F
Hold cooked food at serving temperature	325 - 375 °F
Lamb Steaks	325 - 375 °F
Flattened Boneless Chicken	375 - 400 °F
Vegetables (sliced or grated)	

STEAK DONENESS	INTERNAL TEMPERATURE
EXTRA RARE or "BLUE" • Seared outside • Completely red interior • Cold and soft center	115 - 120 °F
RARE • Seared outside • 75% red interior • Sightly cool center	125 - 130 °F
MEDIUM RARE • Seared outside • 50% red interior • Sightly firm	130 - 140 °F
MEDIUM WELL • Seared outside • Slightest bit of pink in center • Mostly cooked throughout	150 - 155 °F
WELL DONE • Seared outside • Fully brown center • Firm and cooked throughout	160 + °F

Organize the BBQ party of your dreams!